Volume 1

Kingdom Values

by　　　Jon Tyson & Suzy Silk

**Printed by Church of the City New York, in the
United States of America.**

First printing, 2019.

Church of the City New York
409 West 45th st., 5th Floor
New York, NY 10036

church.nyc

Note on Design: This type system is heavily
influenced by some late work by Jan Tschichold,
who is famous among other things for his design
of the original Penguin Books. Although he started
out as a pure-blooded, fiery modernist, much of
his late work—like his layouts for *Typographische
Gestaltung*—integrate more classical typesetting
with the asymmetry and sans-serif styles of
modernism. As a book on the foundations of
Christian values, we wanted to create something
similar—a visual style that felt legible in a modern
context, but still rooted in a rigorous tradition. It's
my hope and prayer God speaks to you through
this small typographic offering. (~Chris)

Typefaces:
GT America, Mrs. Eaves, U.S. 101

Dedication

We couldn't have created this book without the unbelievable support of our church: Church of the City New York. A special thanks to all of the women and men in the Creative Communications Ministry for their help editing, designing, and printing. A special thanks to Tyler Prieb, Christen Smith, Laura Cave, Chris Lo, Megan Carroll, Rebecca Vitkus, Hannah Simpson, Alicia Hosking, Tisza Evans, Haley Wright, Ken Musante, Audrey Elledge, and Elizabeth Moore. May the seeds you have scattered bear a hundredfold.

~ *Suzy*

Table of Contents

§

Introduction

In 21st century America, we find ourselves living in a multi-cultural, post-modern society filled with competing worldviews, diverse religions, self-defined moral systems, and individually created identities. There are a variety of ways to live that are constantly being offered to us—ways to find life, happiness, identity, community, purpose, and the strength to live your "best life." We are offered these ways of life in advertisements, television shows, New York Times' best sellers, work seminars, and fitness classes, and during dinner conversations with friends, family, and co-workers. The Declaration of Independence even states that we have an inalienable right to "life, liberty, and the pursuit of happiness," and so our modern American society latches onto these words with vigor, trying to find a way to live that both answers the deep questions of life and provides us with personal happiness.

But as the writer of Proverbs warn us, there are ways to live that seem right to us from a human perspective, but that ultimately lead to death. How do we avoid these ways and instead choose the road that leads to life offered by Jesus? In Matthew 7:13-14 Jesus warns His disciples to "enter through the narrow gate. For wide is the gate and broad is the road that leads to destruction, and many enter through it. But small is the gate and narrow the road that leads to life, and only a few find it."

In the midst of all of these ways of living,
how do we learn to live in the way of Jesus?

A 2017 Barna study found that "only 17 percent of Christians who consider their faith important and attend church regularly actually have a biblical worldview." What this study demonstrated was that it's possible to regularly attend church, but still be unsure of the teachings of Jesus and how to grow in them in the midst of a culture of competing values. Brooke Hempell, senior Vice President of research for Barna, concluded: "The challenge with competing worldviews is that there are fragments of similarities to some Christian teachings, and some may recognize and latch onto these ideas, not realizing they are distortions of biblical truths... Informed thinking is essential to developing and maintaining a healthy biblical worldview and faith as well as being able to have productive dialogue with those who espouse other beliefs."

The goal of this book is to help you identify five of the central teachings of Jesus, distinguish them from the false ways of life offered by our modern world, and learn to grow in each of them so that you can both individually, and collectively with other believers, walk confidently down the road that leads to abundant life.

You and I are not meant to live lives tossed to and fro by the waves of culture and every wind of doctrine (Eph. 4:14). No! We are called by Jesus to live abundant lives full of freedom, purpose, and joy. This freedom and deep sense of calling only comes by knowing and embodying the teachings of Jesus. We must respond to His invitation to follow Him. Hebrews 3:15 reads, "Today if you hear His voice, do not harden your hearts." Today, Jesus is inviting you to follow Him. Join us, as we study and learn to walk in the ways of Jesus.

Five Core Values

In studying the teachings of Jesus recorded in the New Testament, our church has found it helpful to summarize these teachings into five core values: gospel, identity, community, mission, and power. We believe these five values not only provide a roadmap for many of Jesus' central teachings, but that they also point to a wholistic, integrated way of pursuing the abundant life offered in Jesus; together they stand in stark contrast to the many broken ways of life our world offers to us.

The following chapters will each expand upon a different value and how we, as disciples, can grow in them, but here is a short introduction to get us started.

Chapter 01 ~ **Gospel**

Throughout His ministry, Jesus proclaimed the good news (gospel) of the Kingdom of God. Jesus made the radical claim that abundant life now and eternal life after death were only possible in Him. He, and the writers of the New Testament, described our state apart from Him as being dead, enslaved, and blind to the things of God in our natural state. Apart from faith in His death and resurrection, and indwelling by the Holy Spirit, we are unable to know God or how to live as a follower of Jesus. We are unable to save ourselves, resurrect ourselves, or free ourselves from our broken ways of thinking and living; only Jesus can rescue, redeem, purify, and transform us. The good news is that Jesus offers us salvation and life freely, not based on our works or actions, but purely by faith in Him.

In the midst of a world that tells us "the good life" can be achieved and maintained if we work hard enough, the promise of grace given freely is truly good news. And in a world that offers us no real security either here or after death, Jesus offers us eternal life secured by His works and His eternal power. We do not have to fear death or to strive and fret each day, but instead we can live the full life Jesus came to bring us.

As we learn to walk with Jesus, we can also learn to grow in our understanding of the gospel— both intellectually and experientially. Over time we will find ourselves more and more free from the lies and patterns of our former life as we learn to rest in the good news that we are fully loved and forgiven because of the work of Jesus on our behalf. This freedom will enable us to extend grace to ourselves and to those around us, making us more joyful, free people.

In Chapter 1, we will learn a succinct definition of the gospel and then think through the implications the gospel has upon our lives as individuals and its implications for our entire world.

Chapter 02 ~ **Identity**

As Ravi Zacharias highlighted above, many of the central human longings center on identity questions like *"Who am I?"* and *"Why am I here?"*. As soon as we are born, our parents give us a name. Then as they and our larger community observe and shape our development, these adults might even assign us identity markers based on culturally-defined norms and values. Every culture, in fact, has an identity formation process it

sends us through in order to determine our sense of
self and our sense of value in the world. But every
culturally-defined identity has its flaws and shortcom-
ings, as we will see in Chapter 2, and so we are often
left struggling with isolation, insecurity, and shame.

In stark contrast to the way of the world, God wishes
to give each of us a secure, beautiful identity based
on His righteousness, His acceptance, and His divine
purpose for our life. Through the work of the Triune God,
we can become a child of God, holy and dearly loved.
Instead of striving to live *for* favor and acceptance, we
can live *from* favor and unwavering acceptance. This
new identity then frees us to confess, forgive, live with
integrity, and love freely.

Chapter 03 ~ **Community**

Our God is a triune God who is always in community
with Himself. When God created humankind, He said
that it was not good for man to be alone, and it is why
He gave Adam and Eve together the job of being His
image-bearers on the earth. Since God is three distinct
persons unified in perfect community, only a communal
people can accurately reflect His image well.

The same is still true today. We are not meant to follow
Jesus on our own, but as a community. In contrast
to our culture that emphasizes individualism above
communal life and preference over commitment (see
Chapter 3), our God invites us to join His covenant
people—seeing ourselves as individuals forming a unified whole. This is why the Bible calls us the "people of
God," "the body of Christ," "the royal priesthood," and
"a holy nation." It is in the context of a covenant people

that we can reflect the image of God and join Him in renewing the world.

Chapter 04 ~ **Mission**

As a redeemed people, God invites us to join Him in His good work of bringing His kingdom and renewing our world. This mission involves spiritual renewal (proclaiming the good news of the kingdom so that people can be brought from darkness to light, from enemies of God to children of God), social renewal (tearing down the dividing walls that sin has created between individuals and communities), and cultural renewal (bringing every part of human society under the reign of God, so culture serves to aid in the flourishing of humanity and creation).

Every one of us is sent by Jesus into our world to bring the kingdom, steward the gifts and resources He has given us for human flourishing, and to model His servant-love to those around us. Our mission is to glorify God through our worship and our everyday lives. There is no greater joy in life than to enjoy God's presence and to make Him known.

Chapter 05 ~ **Power**

Jesus never intended for us to live the Christian life and follow Him out of our own strength and power. Even Jesus waited for the Spirit to come upon Him before He launched His ministry. Likewise, Jesus invites us to be filled and empowered by the Spirit each and every day—to experience His intimate presence in our life, to be transformed by Him into His image, to allow the Spirit to bear fruit in and through our life, and to witness the miraculous power of God moving out of us to heal and renew our world.

The fruit, gifts, and power of the Spirit are not meant to be seen in the lives of just a few, unusual, "special" Christians. No, God intends that every believer experience His presence and live out of His supernatural power. Jesus invites us to have life and life abundant through His indwelling Spirit, and to do even greater works than He did (John 14:12). Through His Spirit, God transforms our lives from ordinary lives to extraordinary kingdom-bringing lives.

Our Prayer for You

Whether you are a part of this community for a few weeks, a few months, or the long haul, we hope this framework will guide you as you grow in deeper discipleship and spiritual maturity. Our prayer is that you will:

- Be liberated by understanding the good news of what God has done for you in Jesus (Gospel)
- Become whole and healthy as you flourish in a secure, God-given identity (Identity)
- Belong to and participate in radically loving, formative relationships (Community)
- Find purpose and vision in joining God's restorative work in the world (Mission)
- Learn to rely on and experience the power of God's Spirit within you (Power).

A Model for Growth

As we progress through this book, we will employ a simple model to help us remember the five values, evaluate our current understanding of each value, and track our progress as we grow in each area. This model will also allow us to understand how each value impacts and shapes the others, reminding us that following Jesus is a holistic approach to life that impacts the heart, soul, mind, and strength—or in other words, every part of our life. To grow in one area,

A Model For Growth In Five Stages

❶ Know God's Plan
❷ Experience
❸ Apply
❹ Grow in Confidence
❺ Lived Daily Experience

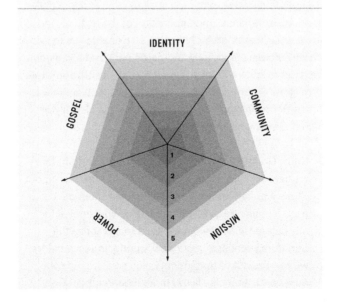

at the deficit of the others, is to become lopsided in our Christian life; but as we seek to grow in each of the five areas together, we will soon discover that each value actually strengthens, pours into, and enables the other values to be fully lived out. We can only have a secure identity as a child of God, when we understand that we are a child because of Jesus' works and not our own (the gospel). And we can only pursue the mission of God effectively, if we are filled with the power of God through the Holy Spirit. To build an identity apart from the gospel, is still a fragile identity; and to live out the mission of God without the power of God will soon lead to burn-out. Each central teaching of Jesus is integrated with all of the others.

As you can see above, we have divided each section of the pentagon into five stages of growth, so you can quickly evaluate where you are and what steps you need to take to grow in that area of life.

In each of these five values we seek to grow in our understanding, experience, and application of the truth of God. As we grow in each area of life, this also enables us to live in the way of Jesus more fully and participate in His kingdom. We need to know the truth, experience the truth, apply the truth, grow in confidence in living this truth out, and have this truth become our lived, daily experience. Here's why each of these is so important.

❶ **Know God's Plan** ~ We need to know the truth before we can live it. By studying the Word, we can learn about God's plan for our lives and begin to have our minds transformed. We need to know the gospel intellectually before we can live it, we need to memorize the Scriptures concerning our new identity in Jesus before we can live out of that identity, and so forth. And the best part is there is always more to learn about God!

❷ **Experience** ~ This knowledge then needs to move out of our head and into our experiences. This often begins by experimenting, praying, and asking God to help you feel, touch, and see the truth of what the Scriptures say. You might decide to join a community group, and for the first time experience the love of other people. Or you might pray for help from God, and experience for the first time the Spirit's power or witness a miracle!

❸ **Apply** ~ Now that you know what your life in God is meant to look like and you have had a few experiences of this new life offered in Jesus, now begins the work of believing and applying this new truth to your life. It involves taking the claims of Scripture and declaring them to be true in your life. It involves stepping out in faith to obey Jesus, believing His way is best. It means leaning into relationships so you can become a part of Jesus' body. It means praying over your friend who is sick, because you believe Jesus can heal.

❹ **Grow in Confidence** ~ As you start living more and more in the way of Jesus, taking greater steps of faith to live these truths out, you will begin to grow in confidence and boldness. You will not only apply the gospel to your own life but you will boldly share it with others. You begin to learn more and more how to rely upon the power of the Spirit, and you will learn to confidently take risks for God's mission.

❺ **Lived Daily Experience** ~ Eventually the truths of the Scripture become your new "normal"—your lived, daily experience looks more and more like the daily life of Jesus who proclaimed the good news, deeply knew His identity as the Son of God, made disciples and invited strangers into the people of God, lived out of the mission God had given Him, and was filled with the power of the Spirit to heal the sick and perform miracles.

As you look at this diagram with its five values and five growth steps, *what is your initial self-assessment? Which step are you on in each triangle?*

At the end of each chapter we will provide a self-assessment tool for that section of the pentagon, along with suggested growth steps. In the final chapter we will return to all five values, creating a personal growth plan to be practiced in the context of a believing community (whether a community group, Bible study, or CORE group).

Getting the Most Out of This Book

In order to get the most out of this book, we highly recommend taking each of the chapter assessments seriously and thoughtfully. Give yourself the time and space to truly evaluate yourself honestly, inviting the Holy Spirit to search you and reveal blind spots and errors in your way of thinking and living. Only the Spirit truly knows the thoughts and intentions of our heart, so allow yourself to be gently sifted and rebuked by Him.

Once you have evaluated yourself, read the growth suggestions for that developmental stage and put these into practice.

Along with taking the assessments, we encourage you to discuss this book with other like-minded believers. Not only discuss the ideas in this book, but invite them to pray for you, ask you questions, and hold you accountable for the decisions the Spirit leads you to make in response to this book. There is a group discussion guide at the end of this book, along with a list of suggested resources.

Finally, each chapter has a guided self-reflection activity based on the acronym **T.I.M.E.** and a relevant passage of Scripture. We encourage you to set aside at least 45 minutes for this practice, so you have ample time to meditate and listen to the Spirit. **T.I.M.E.** is a tool for studying the Bible on a daily basis, designed by Pastor Jon Tyson. The acronym stands for: Text, Immerse, Ministry, and Encounter.

> **Text** ~ Read the Bible and pay attention to anything that the Spirit highlights.

> **Immerse** ~ Study the highlighted verse or phrase, by using various Bible tools/software so you can understand it more deeply. Record anything you learn.

> **Ministry** ~ Ask God how He wants to apply this to your life. How does He want to transform you? What action might He want you to take?

> **Encounter** ~ Take your learning and application to God in prayer. Talk with God and listen to Him. Close your time in worship and adoration. The goal of this time is to enter into the presence of God, laying your cares before Him, being empowered by His Spirit, and worshiping Him for who He is.

Like the apostle James encouraged us, we do not want to be people who merely hear the Word of God, we want to do what it says and to believe it deep in our hearts (James 1:22). Reading this book and acquiring more head knowledge will be a fruitless endeavor; rather, we need to bring the truth of Scripture into the presence of God and ask Him to transform us. It is in prayer and worship in the context of the community of believers that we experience life transformation.

Join us as we seek to live in the way of Jesus together.

01

Gospel

"Jesus' gospel ... contrasts two ways of thinking. The more common version is thought to involve how people ensure they will go to heaven when they die. It's about how to go from 'down here' to 'up there.' ... The other understanding is that the gospel announces the availability of life under God's reign and power now. It's about 'up there' coming 'down here.'"
—John Ortberg

As Christians we can often be guilty of throwing around words that we assume everyone understands, when in reality we often fail to explore or comprehend their true meaning ourselves. One clear example of this trend is the way we use the word "saved." Saved gets batted around in coffee shops, sermons, and small groups, but what does it even mean? Saved from what? Sin? Hell? Myself? This world? Death? Anger? Other people? All of the above? And when does salvation start? We need clarity on this vital word before we can fully embrace the central claim of our faith.

To begin to talk about salvation is to begin by talking about God. He is the one that has planned, accomplished, and secured salvation for us, and He has done this through what Biblical writers called "the gospel." The word gospel was not a term that Christians invented but one they borrowed. Colin Brown of the New International Dictionary of New Testament Theology states:

> *In the Greek New Testament, gospel is the translation of the Greek noun euangelion (occurring 76 times) "good news," and the verb euangelizo (occurring 54 times), meaning "to bring or announce good news." Both words are derived from the noun angelos, "messenger." In classical Greek, an euangelos was one who brought a message of victory or other political or personal news that caused joy. In addition, euangelizomai … meant "to speak as a messenger of gladness, to proclaim good news." Further, the noun euangelion became a technical term for the message of victory, though it was also used for a political or private message that brought joy.*

The first Christians took this Greek term and applied it to their announcement of Jesus' great victory and the arrival of His kingdom, ushered in through His life, death, and resurrection. The Christian gospel is the announcement of the good news of Christ's victory over sin, Satan, death, and hell.

When you hear the term "good news"—what do you think of? When was the last time you received good news? When was the last time you listened to a news anchor or read a newspaper that brought good news?

Sadly, our world is often filled with bad news more than good news. We hear about wars, disease, addictions, political corruption, violence, and tragedy on a daily basis. And often this news can lead us to become disheartened, disillusioned, or even desensitized. In the midst of this despondency and disillusionment, we can start to manufacture our own shallow, temporary versions of "good news."

False News

Since the fall of our ancient ancestors, Adam and Eve, human beings have had a propensity to try and save them—selves from their own brokenness through human effort. This can manifest itself in personal piety, philanthropy, morality, or religious claims about other ways to God. At their root, false religious gospels depend on human effort and skewed views of God. They often make alternative claims of special revelation and truth that have been forgotten or rediscovered. Paul warned the Galatians about this danger when he wrote: "But even if we or an angel from heaven should preach a gospel other than the one we preached to you, let them be under God's curse! As we have already said, so now I say again: If anybody is preaching to you a gospel other than what you accepted, let them be under God's curse!" (Gal 1:8–9) Modern examples of this include the Jehovah's Witnesses, Mormons, Scientology, Kabbalah, and many other religious sects.

Secular salvation is a gospel of false promises built around worldly versions of independence and success. This is the "good news" of self-fulfillment, success, power, wealth, sexuality, and autonomy. Secularism offers to save us from insignificance, loneliness, boredom, and meaninglessness. It offers a false vision of the future built upon an identity affirmed by the world, fleeting pleasures that don't last, and resources with the power to eliminate the problems that plague our personal lives. This gospel cannot deliver true salvation. Success is temporary at best—beauty fades, sex stops, and popular approval shifts. Secularism produces an exhausting need to keep up or you'll be swept aside by the hungry masses. Rather than offering life, secularism kills our spirits and alienates us from God and one another.

False gospels offering false salvation radically overpromise and underdeliver. Their fruit is slavery and not freedom. Paul addresses this again to the Galatians when he writes: "Formerly, when you did not know God, you were slaves to those who by nature are not gods. But now that you know God—or rather are known by God—how is it that you are turning back to those weak and miserable forces? Do you wish to be enslaved by them all over again?" (Gal 4:8–9) The salvation God offers us is about freedom and joy, and not about slavery. He came to meet the deepest longings of our hearts that can only be satisfied and fulfilled in Him.

In stark contrast to these worldly strategies, the Bible makes the radical claim that it indeed has good news to offer and that this good news regards not just the present or the individual person, but that it is good news for all time and for all people. This is why 2,000 years ago a large crowd of angels startled a group of sleeping shepherds with the bold proclamation: "Today in the town of David a Savior has been born to you; he is the Messiah, the Lord. This will be a sign to you: You will find a baby wrapped in cloths and lying in a manger" (Luke 2:11–12).

So what is this good news that the angels proclaimed and that the first Christians willingly gave their lives to declare?

If we were to look at the current life of the average American church-goer, their lives don't seem to be much different from anyone else's! If anything, the people who attend church seem to have lives that closely resemble the rest of the country. One reason for this disparity is that we, as Christians, have lost track of the gospel, the message of the good news. We are like a group of children playing "telephone" in which the secret message at the end of the line sounds nothing like the initial message. Recent Barna studies have found that 60% of Americans who identify as Christian do not regularly attend church, pray, or read their Bibles, and that many Christians have taken beliefs from other religions and schools of thought that are seamlessly integrated into their own thinking—often without ever realizing that these views are in sharp contrast to the truths found in the Bible. As Brooke Hempell, senior VP of research for Barna asserts: "The call for the Church, and its teachers and thinkers, is to help Christians dissect popular beliefs before allowing them to settle in their own ideology."

If Christians do not know what the gospel is, they cannot live out of this good news. If we have distorted or watered-down definitions of the gospel, our lives will not be full of the life, joy, peace, and power that Jesus promised to His disciples. Seeking to grow in our understanding and not settling for a shallow faith is crucial to the Christian life. Hebrews 5:11–14 makes clear the importance of intentionality in our knowledge of God:

> *We have much to say about this, but it is hard to make it clear to you because you no longer try to understand. In fact, though by this time you ought to be teachers, you need someone to teach you the elementary truths of God's word all over again. You need milk, not solid food! Anyone who lives on milk, being still an infant, is not acquainted with the teaching about righteousness. But solid food is for the mature, who by constant use have trained themselves to distinguish good from evil.*

With this in mind, let's choose to move beyond infantile understandings of faith, and instead lay a solid foundational understanding of the gospel upon which we can build our lives.

The Historical Faith

In past generations, when average Christians did not have access to read the gospel and the truths of Scripture, or when a large percentage of the population was illiterate, Church leadership formed short memorable creeds that would summarize the truths of the faith. The two most famous of these, which are still memorized by many Christians today, are the Apostles' Creed and the Nicene Creed.

The Apostles' Creed was written in the form we now know it in 710–714 CE. It was based on a short text, the Old Roman Creed, which was created sometime before 340 CE and was credited to the twelve apostles in church history. The text of the Apostles' Creed reads as follows:

> *I believe in God, the Father Almighty,*
> *the Creator of heaven and earth,*
> *and in Jesus Christ, His only Son, our Lord:*
> *Who was conceived of the Holy Spirit,*
> *born of the Virgin Mary,*
> *suffered under Pontius Pilate,*
> *was crucified, died, and was buried.*
> *He descended to the dead.*
> *The third day He arose again from the dead.*
> *He ascended into heaven*
> *and sits at the right hand of God the Father Almighty,*
> *whence He shall come to judge the living and the dead.*
> *I believe in the Holy Spirit, the holy universal church,*
> *the communion of saints,*
> *the forgiveness of sins,*
> *the resurrection of the body,*
> *and life everlasting.*

The Nicene Creed was written in 325 CE at the First Council of Nicaea, and then was lengthened in 381 CE at the First Council of Constantinople. It reads:

*I believe in one God, the Father Almighty, Maker of heaven
and earth, and of all things visible and invisible.
And in one Lord Jesus Christ, the only-begotten Son of God,
begotten of the Father before all worlds;
God of God, Light of Light, very God of very God;
begotten, not made, being of one substance with the Father,
by whom all things were made.
Who, for us men for our salvation, came down from heaven,
and was incarnate by the Holy Spirit of the virgin Mary,
and was made man;
and was crucified also for us under Pontius Pilate;
He suffered and was buried;
and the third day He rose again, according to the Scriptures;
and ascended into heaven, and sits on the right hand of the Father;
and He shall come again, with glory, to judge the quick
and the dead;
whose kingdom shall have no end.
And I believe in the Holy Ghost, the Lord and Giver of Life;
who proceeds from the Father and the Son;
who with the Father and the Son together is worshipped and
glorified;
who spoke by the prophets.
And I believe in one holy catholic and apostolic Church. I
acknowledge one baptism for the remission of sins;
and I look for the resurrection of the dead, and the life of the world
to come.
Amen.*

Each of these creeds sought to crystalize the central message of the gospel in language their generation could understand in order to combat the many lies and common heresies of the day. In this same spirit, our church has put together a short two-sentence summary of the gospel to help us remember the truths of Scripture. We encourage you to begin by memorizing this short paragraph, and then over time, add to this definition the longer Apostles' and Nicene Creeds.

> *The gospel is the good news that God our Father, the Creator, out of His great love for us, has come to rescue us from sin, Satan, death and hell, and to renew all things, in and through the work of Jesus Christ on our behalf, to establish His kingdom, through His people, in the power of the Holy Spirit. This is for God's great glory, and our profound joy.*

You will notice several things about this definition.

- **This is news.** The work of salvation is something that must be announced and discovered. The world did not invent the gospel or discover it within its own wisdom or philosophy. God announced this good news through Jesus, who lived and proclaimed this Gospel, and we proclaim it when we follow in his footsteps.

- **The gospel is about God.** It is the good news of the Father, Son and Spirit working together to plan, accomplish, apply and empower our salvation for us.

- **It is substitutionary.** Jesus bore the punishment for our sin, giving us salvation as a gift, not something we can earn on our own behalf. This is a gospel of grace and not human works. When we trust in Christ through faith, His work becomes our inheritance, position, and standing.

- **It is holistic in its scope.** The gospel includes individual salvation, reconciliation between people, and ultimately the renewal of all creation. We are saved completely—from sin; from Satan, our ancient enemy; from death, the consequence of sin; and from hell, eternal separation from God.

- **It's the gospel of the kingdom.** Its ultimate goal is seeing the Lordship of Jesus established in all of life and into eternity.

- **The gospel is entrusted to us.** We get to partner with God in living out, enjoying, and sharing this good news with others.

- **It is animated by the Holy Spirit's power.** Salvation does not depend upon human wisdom, morality, gifts, philosophy, or strategy. The gospel comes from God, is accomplished by God, and is empowered by His Spirit.

- **It is a gospel of love.** It reveals to us God's desire to redeem a people for Himself, who love and reflect His goodness and glory, and who will enjoy Him forever.

Let's lean into some of the phrases in our gospel definition in more detail, so we can grasp their true and comprehensive implications.

God's News

First the Gospel is *God's* good news—it is news that comes from Him, was created by Him, and declares the work He has done. It is about His victory and kingdom. The good news comes from our Triune God, who collectively created the world and is also collectively redeeming and renewing the world. The God of the Bible is one God, in three persons, who accomplishes His plan for the world in perfect unity

Now when it comes to understanding God, the Christian faith has historically taught that the Christian God is the Trinity, one God in three persons. It is important to note that this word is not actually found in the Bible, but is used to describe what is taught in the Scriptures about the divinity of the Father, Son, and Spirit. The Father is God (1 Cor. 8:6; 1 Pet. 1:3). The Son is God (1 Tim. 6:15; John 8:58; Heb. 1:8). The Holy Spirit is God (Acts 5:3–4; John 3:5–8). This view of God actually sets Christianity apart from all other views of God in the world. Millard Erickson in Introducing Christian Doctrine writes, "In the doctrine of the Trinity, we encounter one of the truly distinctive doctrines of Christianity. Among the religions of the world, the Christian faith is unique in making the claim that God is one and yet there are three who are God." So, what are the core elements of this teaching?

The doctrine of the Trinity means that there is one God who eternally exists as three distinct Persons—the Father, Son, and Holy Spirit. Stated differently, God is one in essence and three in person. What seems like a paradox is possible only because the three are so perfectly united in love. These definitions express three crucial truths:

1. The Father, Son, and Holy Spirit are distinct Persons.
2. Each Person is fully God.
3. There is only one God.

Each of the persons of the Trinity has a specific role to play in redemption: God the Father initiates the plan of salvation out of His great love for us and for His triune glory. God the Son is the promised Savior, the Anointed One (Messiah), who came to live a perfect life on our behalf, then died a terrible death in our place (taking upon Himself the sins of the world), and then rose to life victorious to give us eternal life and inaugurate His kingdom on earth. It is Jesus' work on our behalf that saves, not our own works. Finally, it is the Holy Spirit who works in and through the redeemed people of God. He empowers us, guides us, and produces the fruit of the Spirit in us so that we join God in His renewal of all things. He is the seal upon our hearts that guarantees us eternal life and an inheritance in God's kingdom.

The Gospel is first and foremost about the heart of God, which desires to restore all things for His glory and our good.

This News is GOOD

Two thousand years ago, on that fateful night, the angels began their declaration to the scared shepherds with: "Do not be afraid. I bring you good news that will cause great joy for all the people" (Luke 2:10). The primary description of the news sent by God was good news that would be so good that it would in fact cause *great joy for all people.*

Likewise, when Jesus began His ministry, He declared the good news that God's kingdom was at hand, and that everything the Jewish people had been longing for would finally come to pass. This is why, in Luke 4, at the start of His ministry, Jesus stood up in His local synagogue and read from the scroll of Isaiah:

> *"The Spirit of the Lord is on me, because he has anointed me to proclaim good news to the poor. He has sent me to proclaim freedom for the prisoners and recovery of sight for the blind, to set the oppressed free, to proclaim the year of the Lord's favor." Then he rolled up the scroll, gave it back to the attendant and sat down. The eyes of everyone in the synagogue were fastened on him. 21 He began by saying to them, "Today this scripture is fulfilled in your hearing." (Luke 4:18–21)*

Declaring that the "year of the Lord's favor" had begun certainly sounds like good news to our modern ears, but to His first-century audience the promise of Isaiah 61 was not simply about favor from God, it was about the beginning of the "year of jubilee."

The year of jubilee was a holiday instituted by God in Leviticus 25:8–54. Every 50 years the Israelites were to declare a year of freedom, restoration, and celebration. No work of any kind was to be performed the whole year, all indentured servants were declared free and released from debt, and every piece of land purchased or lost to debt in the past fifty years was to be returned to the original family that owned it. During this year, God would richly provide for the people as they faithfully restored equality, freedom, and rest to their country. In the Jewish mind, the year of jubilee meant redemption and favor; and yet, as far as historians can tell, the year of jubilee was never actually celebrated during the many centuries of Israel's political autonomy.

When Jesus arrives on the scene, the Jewish people are under Roman rule and are longing for God to bring about a jubilee year when they can finally be free. This is exactly the news Jesus is bringing—good news that He is going to release the prisoner, provide for the hungry, and heal the sick. This is not news of God's judgment, but news of God's mercy and favor.

Throughout His ministry, Jesus continues to build upon this joyous theme in the way that He lives and teaches. Jesus is daily feeding the hungry, healing the sick, and freeing the demonically oppressed. He also brings good news to all people by spending time with those society considered unrighteous or unclean; Jesus was accused of dining too much with "prostitutes and sinners." Many of

Jesus' parables are stories about parties: the wedding feast, the banquet, and the three "lost" parables that all end with the person finding the lost item and then throwing a party! (Luke 15) The consistent message Jesus gives is that God wants to throw a party and invite people to this celebration; He wants to find the lost and bring them into His kingdom with great rejoicing. "In the same way, I tell you, there is rejoicing in the presence of the angels of God over one sinner who repents" (Luke 15:10).

To hear God's news and to receive it into your heart is to discover firsthand the goodness, joy, and love of our Creator God towards us. Blaise Pascal, a famous seventeenth-century mathematician, philosopher, and inventor had an encounter with the goodness of God, which profoundly marked his life. He recorded this encounter in a poem that he sewed into the lining of his coat over his heart, which was found upon his death. It beautifully explains the good-ness of the gospel, and began as follows:

> *From about half past ten at night until about half past midnight,*
> *FIRE.*
> *GOD of Abraham, GOD of Isaac, GOD of Jacob*
> *not of the philosophers and of the learned.*
> *Certitude. Certitude. Feeling. Joy. Peace.*
> *GOD of Jesus Christ.*
> *My God and your God.*
> *Your GOD will be my God.*
> *Forgetfulness of the world and of everything, except GOD.*
> *He is only found by the ways taught in the Gospel.*
> *Grandeur of the human soul.*
> *Righteous Father, the world has not known you, but I have known you.*
> *Joy, joy, joy, tears of joy.*

This is God's desire for every single one of us—that the love of God would chase us down, inspire us, and recruit our whole lives. God's goodness and His unfailing love are meant to follow us, chase us, pursue us all the days of our lives (Ps. 23:6). Joy, joy, joy, tears of joy.

Out of His Love: 4 Part Story

When we learn that the gospel begins with God, we are reminded that the good news begins in the heart of God out of His profound love for the Trinity and humanity.

In the past 100 years, and at other times in Church history, the Church has lost the full message of the gospel and has instead relied upon a partial story. This is the "hell-fire and brimstone" story in which people are told they are terrible sinners and they need to repent and be forgiven. Although this story has kernels of truth, it is just part of the story. When we look at the whole narrative of the Bible, from Genesis 1 to Revelation 22, we see the full picture.

This is often referred to as a four- or five-part story. This story begins at the creation of the world, in the heart of God. The first thing we learn is that we were created from and for love. Next, we learn that all humanity has fallen short of God's good purposes, sinning and becoming severed from intimacy with God and others. Then we are told that in the midst of our separation, God began His plan to redeem us by creating a covenant with Abraham promising that through His descendants (the nation of Israel) God would send a savior. This plan of Redemption would culminate in the life, death, and resurrection of Jesus—God in the flesh—who would save us and forgive us. But the good news does not stop there! No, God is not merely saving us from sin and death, but He wants to restore us and invite us into the good work of restoring all things. One day Jesus will return and bring a new heaven and a new earth, and we will once again live with God in perfect intimacy and love.

Rescued From

When we learn that Jesus was called Savior and Messiah, we might rightly ask—what did Jesus rescue us from? In our definition we find that Jesus rescued us from sin, Satan, death, and hell.

Sin

When Jesus rescued us from sin, He saved us from its penalty, power, and presence.

> **Penalty:** 2 Corinthians 5:19 reads: "God was reconciling the world to himself in Christ, not counting people's sins against them;" and Romans 6:23 states, "For the wages of sin is death, but the gift of God is eternal life in Christ Jesus our Lord." Jesus rescued us from the penalty of sin—death and separation from God—that we rightly deserved.

> **Power:** Romans 6:11, 14, 18 reads: "In the same way, count yourselves dead to sin but alive to God in Christ Jesus.... For sin shall no longer be your master, because you are not under the law, but under grace.... You have been set free from sin and have become slaves to righteousness." Through Jesus, we are released from the bondage of sin, which kept us enslaved since birth. This is what Jesus meant when announcing the year of the Lord's favor—he has come to set the captives free. We are free from the power of sin to know and love God.

Presence: Finally, in the book of Revelation the apostle John sees a vision of the promised future:

> *Then I saw "a new heaven and a new earth," for the first heaven and the first earth had passed away, and there was no longer any sea. ...Look! God's dwelling place is now among the people, and he will dwell with them. They will be his people, and God himself will be with them and be their God. 'He will wipe every tear from their eyes. There will be no more death' or mourning or crying or pain, for the old order of things has passed away. ...No longer will there be any curse. (Rev. 21:1, 3b–4, 22:3a)*

Right now we still live in a world where Satan and sin are present and active. We live in a broken world of systemic injustice and unrighteousness, even though as Christians, we are no longer slaves to sin. Ultimately, Jesus will return and cleanse the world of all sin, injustice, and sorrow. In the meantime, through His people, God's kingdom is currently advancing, shining light in the dark corners of our world until all the earth is rid of the presence of wickedness.

Satan

The Bible declares that Jesus rescued us from Satan. In our modern age, people often scoff at or downplay the role of Satan in our world, but the Bible and Jesus Himself are very clear about the identity and role of Satan. Jesus called Satan: "the enemy" (Matt. 13:39), "the evil one" (Matt. 13:38), "the prince of this world" (John 12:31; 14:30), "a liar," "the father of lies," and "a murderer" (John 8:44).

If we do not acknowledge the part Satan plays in our world, we are tempted to make other people the enemy and to vilify and demonize them; but again, Ephesians 6 is clear that "our struggle is not against flesh and blood, but against the rulers, against the authorities, against the powers of this dark world and against the spiritual forces of evil in the heavenly realms" (Eph. 6:12).

The good news of the gospel is that Jesus defeated Satan through His death on the cross. Colossians 2:15 says: "And having disarmed the powers and authorities, he made a public spectacle of them, triumphing over them by the cross." As followers of Jesus we no longer have to fear Satan and his demons because "all authority in heaven and on earth has been given to [Jesus]" (Matt. 28:18). This is why in Luke 10:18–19 Jesus says to His disciples: "I saw Satan fall like lightning from heaven. I have given you authority to trample on snakes and scorpions and to overcome all the power of the enemy; nothing will harm you."

Death & Hell

Finally, Jesus rescued us from the death we rightly deserved because of sin. The Bible states that we were by nature "children of wrath" deserving of God's punishment, and eternal separation from Him in Hell. Through His death, Jesus died on our behalf, and through His perfect life, Jesus gives us His perfect righteousness so that instead of receiving God's wrath and being sent to Hell (a place devoid of God and all goodness), we are given eternal life and invited to forever live with God, in His presence, in the perfect new heavens and new earth (Rev. 21:1).

In the end, the Bible says that Satan, Death, and Hell will be judged and forever defeated. Revelation 20:10, 14 reads: "And the devil, who deceived them, was thrown into the lake of burning sulfur...[to] be tormented day and night for

ever and ever. ...Then death and Hades were thrown into
the lake of fire. The lake of fire is the second death."

To Renew All Things

God rescued us because of His love for us and because
He is renewing all things through the work of Jesus and
the power of the Spirit. He is renewing individual people,
creating a new redeemed people, and establishing His
kingdom on earth as it is in heaven.

Renewing Individual People

When Jesus began His ministry, He read these famous
words from the book of Isaiah: "The Spirit of the Lord is on
me, because he has anointed me to proclaim good news
to the poor. He has sent me to proclaim freedom for the
prisoners and recovery of sight for the blind, to set the
oppressed free, to proclaim the year of the Lord's favor."
(Luke 4:18–19). At the start of His ministry, Jesus declared
that the purpose of His coming was to declare the year of
the Lord's favor when those who were far from God (the
spiritually poor, blind, and oppressed) would be forgiven,
washed, and brought into God's kingdom. This is why, when
speaking to a religious leader, Jesus said: "No one can enter
the kingdom of God unless they are born of water and the
Spirit. Flesh gives birth to flesh, but the Spirit gives birth to
spirit. You should not be surprised at my saying, 'You must
be born again.' ...For God so loved the world that he gave
his one and only Son, that whoever believes in him shall not
perish but have eternal life" (John 3:5–7, 16). Jesus clearly
states that what humanity needs most is to be born again, to
experience a spiritual birth, and this birth comes by believing in Jesus and receiving the promised Holy Spirit.

Spiritual birth is not something we earn or can achieve ourselves, it is something done by the Spirit alone. In a culture often built upon human effort and human performance, Jesus' message that we are spiritually dead and unable to revive ourselves can feel shocking.

Paul explains God's process of renewing individual people in his letter to the Ephesian church. Paul begins by stating:

> *As for you, you were dead in your transgressions and sins, in which you used to live when you followed the ways of this world and of the ruler of the kingdom of the air, the spirit who is now at work in those who are disobedient. All of us also lived among them at one time, gratifying the cravings of our flesh and following its desires and thoughts. Like the rest, we were by nature deserving of wrath. (Eph. 2:1–3)*

In short: All of us are made up of a body, soul/mind, and spirit; and because of sin, every person is born with a dead spirit that is unable to know God, comprehend divine things, or live in any way other than as a slave to sin.

Paul continues, "But because of his great love for us, God, who is rich in mercy, made us alive with Christ even when we were dead in transgressions—it is by grace you have been saved" (Eph. 2:4-5). Through Jesus, our once dead spirits are made alive to the things of God. We cannot resurrect our own dead spirits, only Jesus can do this miraculous work for us!

Not only are our spirits made alive, Paul then explains that we are given a new status and identity:

> *And God raised us up with Christ and seated us with him in the heavenly realms in Christ Jesus, in order that in the*

coming ages he might show the incomparable riches of his grace, expressed in his kindness to us in Christ Jesus. For it is by grace you have been saved, through faith—and this is not from yourselves, it is the gift of God—not by works, so that no one can boast. For we are God's handiwork, created in Christ Jesus to do good works, which God prepared in advance for us to do. (Eph. 2:6–10)

The first renewing work God does is to bring individual people from death to life, from being dead to God to being alive in Christ, from being slaves to sin to being freed children of God. Although Jesus did care for people's external needs—by healing the sick and performing miracles—these external works were ultimately meant to address deeper emotional and spiritual needs. More than being healed from their physical illnesses, Jesus wanted to heal their hearts and revive their souls. This is why Jesus spent his time making disciples who could carry the gospel message instead of working to overthrow the Roman government. Jesus knew that any lasting social or cultural changes would flow out of spiritual renewal. As Dallas Willard in *Renovation of the Heart* explains:

The revolution of Jesus is first and always a revolution of the human heart. His revolution does not proceed through the means of social institutions and laws—the outer forms of our existence—intending that these would then impose a good order of life upon people who come under their power. Rather, his is a revolution of character, which proceeds by changing people from the inside through ongoing personal relationship with God and one another. It is a revolution that changes people's ideas, beliefs, feelings, and habits of choice, as well as their bodily tendencies and social relations. It penetrates to the deepest layers of their soul. External, social arrangements may be useful to this end, but they are not the end, nor are they a fundamental part of the means.

Creating a Redeemed People

Along with bringing individual people from death to life, God also longs to create one unified redeemed people out of these varied individuals. The apostle Peter wrote of God's plan to create a redeemed people for Himself: "But you are a chosen people, a royal priesthood, a holy nation, God's special possession, that you may declare the praises of him who called you out of darkness into his wonderful light. Once you were not a people, but now you are the people of God; once you had not received mercy, but now you have received mercy" (1 Peter 2:9–10).

Jesus invites us to become a unified people no longer divided by the world's hostilities but united by the love of Christ. When our world seeks to divide us into groups by industry, neighborhood, wealth, gender, ethnicity, or age, Jesus makes us into a diverse, yet unified group of people. In this way Jesus forms a new humanity, a new nation, a new family, and a new Temple all rooted and grounded in Christ. The social renewal, peace, and unity our world longs for, but is unable to achieve through social reform or legislation, can be accomplished through the radical work of Jesus Christ.

Establishing His Kingdom

Jesus begins His ministry by announcing that "the time has come; the kingdom of God has come near" (Mark 1:15). As Dallas Willard so beautifully summarizes: "Kingdoms are about 'the range of effective will'—the space where you get what you want done, and you have the right and power to get what you want done. In fact, if we are honest, we each try to be the king of our own small kingdom—trying to extend the range of our effective will even when it comes into conflict with another person's range of effective will!"

To the first-century Jewish mind, "the kingdom of God" was God's rule and reign on the earth. This kingdom had practical implications for all of life because God Himself would be the king of His people. In God's future kingdom, Israel's enemies would be defeated, the promised Messiah would sit on David's throne and there would be true shalom—wholeness, happiness, security, and an end to all strife.

When Jesus began to preach, he redefined the arrival of the kingdom, entrance into the kingdom, and how the kingdom would advance on earth. First, he made the radical claim that the kingdom had arrived already by claiming to be the promised Messiah who would usher in God's kingdom and bring peace to the human heart. Second, Jesus redefined entrance into God's kingdom by saying that it was not based on lineage or personal righteousness, but instead was based on rebirth through faith in Him and renewal by the Spirit! Anyone could enter God's kingdom through faith and begin living in God's kingdom, because entrance is based on His lineage (not ours) and upon His righteousness (not ours). Finally, Jesus taught that the extension of God's kingdom would be through the Holy Spirit filling His disciples. Through the work of the Spirit in the lives of believers, the kingdom would be seen on earth as it is in heaven.

Jesus announced and ushered in God's kingdom—His rule and reign on the earth through His Spirit working in His people. The advance of God's kingdom begins in the human heart but then extends to all of the earth; God makes all things new.

The arrival of God's kingdom was good news to the
first-century Jewish world, and it should be good news
to us. The prophet Isaiah's later writings describe what
the world will be like when God reigns as king. There will
be salvation, righteousness and justice, peace, joy, God's
presence, healing, and a return from "exile." When God
establishes His kingdom, every sector of society benefits,
and there is both human and natural flourishing. We see
this promised in Isaiah 65:17–25:

> "See, I will create new heavens and a new earth. The former things
> will not be remembered, nor will they come to mind. But be glad and
> rejoice forever in what I will create, for I will create Jerusalem to be
> a delight and its people a joy. I will rejoice over Jerusalem and take
> delight in my people; the sound of weeping and of crying will be heard
> in it no more. "Never again will there be in it an infant who lives but
> a few days, or an old man who does not live out his years; the one
> who dies at a hundred will be thought a mere child; the one who fails
> to reach a hundred will be considered accursed. They will build houses
> and dwell in them; they will plant vineyards and eat their fruit. No
> longer will they build houses and others live in them, or plant and
> others eat. For as the days of a tree, so will be the days of my people;
> my chosen ones will long enjoy the work of their hands. They will not
> labor in vain, nor will they bear children doomed to misfortune; for
> they will be a people blessed by the Lord, they and their descendants
> with them. Before they call I will answer; while they are still speaking
> I will hear. The wolf and the lamb will feed together, and the lion will
> eat straw like the ox, and dust will be the serpent's food. They will
> neither harm nor destroy on all my holy mountain," says the Lord.

For His Glory & Our Joy

Finally, as we reflect upon our summarized definition of
the gospel, we see that the good news begins in love and
ends in glory and joy. God accomplishes all of His work in

us and in our world for His glory and our joy. What is God's glory? It's the rightful praise and worship He deserves because of who He is (His holiness, perfect love and justice, His wisdom) and what He has done (creating the world, redeeming the world, sustaining the world). God is rightly to be praised, and as people created to praise Him and revel in His beauty, we are most joyful when we are worshipping in His presence. As John Piper wrote, "God is most glorified in us when we are most satisfied in Him." Or as the Psalmist wrote in 73:25–26, 28: "Whom have I in heaven but you? And earth has nothing I desire besides you. My flesh and my heart may fail, but God is the strength of my heart and my portion forever. ...it is good to be near God. I have made the Sovereign Lord my refuge; I will tell of all your deeds."

Growing in your Identity

Even after initially believing the gospel and receiving Jesus into your life as Lord, it is still so important to meditate upon the truth of the gospel. We need to daily remind ourselves of the truth that we are forgiven, redeemed, justified, and sanctified because of Jesus' work on the cross and the indwelling of the Spirit. Growing in our knowledge of and the appropriation of the gospel is a life-long journey of new mercy and freedom each day.

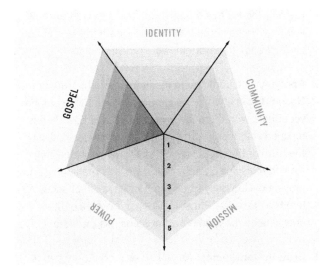

Based on your initial self-evaluation in the introduction, here are some practical next steps for growing in the Gospel.

❶ **Know God's Plan:** If the ideas in this chapter are new to you, then the best place to start is by memorizing the short definition of the gospel and memorizing some of the key verses shared in this chapter. You might want to write these verses out in your journal and hang them on the walls of your apartment. Also, think through the implications of the gospel upon your life and write out your story/testimony. Share your story with someone this week.

❷ **Experience:** If the ideas in this chapter are not new to you, then consider being baptized. This is a way to publicly declare what God has done in your life, and this is a beautiful experience that will mark your life. Before and after your baptism, invite the Holy Spirit to work in you, transforming you from your old way of life and into the holy life He has brought you into. Ask God to show you how He has brought you from death to life, and how He is already transforming you into His image.

❸ **Apply:** As you continue to meditate upon the truth of the Gospel, begin sharing the good news with those around you. Share with them the love of Jesus and how He has rescued you. Along with evangelism, practice applying the truth of the gospel to your daily life by confessing sin and receiving God's forgiveness, by worshipping and praying to God daily since you now have direct access into His presence. Prayerfully resist the work of the enemy because you know that Jesus has the victory!

❹ **Grow in Confidence:** As you grow in confidence in the gospel, learn to boldly share the gospel with friends and family, to quickly confess sin and receive forgiveness, to quickly go to God in prayer and worship, to take captive every thought and every spirit that is in opposition to Christ, and to rely upon the Spirit every moment so that your life is filled with increasing amounts of love, joy, peace, patience, kindness, goodness, gentleness, and self-control.

Self Reflection:
John 3

This week use T.I.M.E.,
described in the Introduction,
with John 3.

John 3:1–19, (NIV)

[1]Now there was a Pharisee, a man named Nicodemus who was a member of the Jewish ruling council. [2] He came to Jesus at night and said, "Rabbi, we know that you are a teacher who has come from God. For no one could perform the signs you are doing if God were not with him." [3] Jesus replied, "Very truly I tell you, no one can see the kingdom of God unless they are born again." [4] "How can someone be born when they are old?" Nicodemus asked. "Surely they cannot enter a second time into their mother's womb to be born!"[5] Jesus answered, "Very truly I tell you, no one can enter the kingdom of God unless they are born of water and the Spirit. [6] Flesh gives birth to flesh, but the Spirit gives birth to spirit. [7] You should not be surprised at my saying, 'You must be born again.' [8] The wind blows wherever it pleases. You hear its sound, but you cannot tell where it comes from or where it is going. So it is with everyone born of the Spirit." [9] "How can this be?" Nicodemus asked. [10] "You are Israel's teacher," said Jesus, "and do you not understand these things? [11] Very truly I tell you, we speak of what we know, and we testify to what we have seen, but still you people do not accept our testimony. [12] I have spoken to you of earthly things and you do not believe; how then will you believe if I speak of heavenly things? [13] No one has ever gone into heaven except the one who came from heaven—the Son of Man. [14] Just as Moses lifted up the snake in the wilderness, so the Son of Man must be lifted up, [15] that everyone who believes may have eternal life in him." [16] For God so loved the world that he gave his one and only Son, that whoever believes in him shall not perish but have eternal life. [17] For God did not send his Son into the world to condemn the world, but to save the world through him. [18] Whoever believes in him is not condemned, but whoever does not believe stands condemned already because they have not believed in the name of God's one and only Son. [19] This is the verdict: Light has come into the world, but people loved darkness instead of light because their deeds were evil.

Text

Read through the passage three times. Underline or highlight any words or phrases that jump out to you.

What does this passage teach about the gospel?
(List those verses or phrases below.)

Immerse

Choose two or three phrases or verses to study further. You might want to look up the definition for those words, find out where those Greek words are used elsewhere in the Scriptures, or study the theological and historical context for those verses. Write a summary of your findings below, and then choose one verse to memorize this week.

PHRASE A:

INSIGHT:

PHRASE B:

INSIGHT:

PHRASE C:

INSIGHT:

MEMORY VERSE:

Ministry

Now that you have read and studied the text, what is the Spirit leading you to believe or do as a result? Why did the Spirit highlight those phrases or words? What is He trying to teach you about the gospel? How is He calling you to live and act as a result?

Encounter

With all of this in mind, take this to God in prayer. Use the space below to write out a prayer and also to write out anything you hear God saying as a result. Then close your time by writing out a song/poem of praise to God.

MY PRAYER:

LISTENING:

MY SONG OF PRAISE:

02

Identity

"In the social jungle of human existence, there is no feeling of being alive without a sense of identity."
— *Erik Erikson*

When you and I were born, we were not born into a neutral space. Rather, we were born into a river—a cultural space with currents that formed and deformed our very identities. Whether we consciously realize it or not, "every culture, without our permission and without naming it as such, imposes an identity formation process on us, its members" (Tim Keller). From the moment we are born, we find ourselves in the midst of a culture that forms us in a certain way, teaching us to get our sense of who we are and why we are valuable from certain things. Our very thoughts about ourselves and why we matter, and what we must do and be to matter, are all shaped by our cultural and social environments.

No matter how wonderful or how challenging this process was as we grew up, as Christians seeking to live in the way of Jesus, it is important for us to recognize and deconstruct the sense of self we carry from our culture and bring that into the light of the teachings of Jesus. *How is our culture forming our identity and how does Jesus want to form (or re-form) our identity?*

Identity Formation

When we seek to answer the question, "Who am I?" our name and genealogy will not suffice. Instead our identity is our "sense of self and sense of worth; it's our core trust and our source of value and recognition. ... It's whatever [we] look to as the ultimate source of our security and worth" (Keller). Put another way, our identity is "defined by the commitments and identifications which provide the frame or horizon within which I can try to determine from case to case what is good, or valuable, or what ought to be done or what I endorse or oppose" (Taylor).

If identity formation is based on a framework of what is good, beautiful, and valuable and how a person measures up to that good, then we must first recognize that every culture creates and gives us a framework within which to form our identities. This framework allows us to make the daily decisions of life, telling us "what is good or bad, what is worth doing, what has meaning and importance for you, and what is trivial and secondary" (Taylor). An identity is our sense of self within a larger framework that gives us worth and value; and likewise, an identity crisis occurs when we lose that framework, and no longer have a sense of self-worth or guiding principles by which to make daily decisions.

But what is the framework within which our identities are formed? To answer this question fully for our current time period, it is helpful to look at a brief synopsis of identity formation throughout human history and into the present. (For a fuller examination of this topic, read Charles Taylor's *Sources of the Self* which describes the shift from "traditional" and "modern" identities in greater detail.)

Traditional and Modern Identities[1]

In ancient times, a person's identity was formed within a traditional, honor-based framework. Living an honorable life was defined as the highest good, and being an honorable person meant that you had a secure, valued, and affirmed identity. Most cultures defined honor as sacrificing one's own happiness and life for the sake of a community, for the sake of others. If the community survived, grew, and thrived as a result of your efforts and life, then you were an honorable person and worthy of praise.

This ancient, traditional identity was a completely external identity. Honor was defined by the community as the highest good, and it was the community, family, and parents who determined if you had lived up to this good. Your job was to learn the definition of honor and then seek to live according to it, to get your thoughts, desires, and feelings to submit to living an honorable life for the sake of others.

During the 500s–300s BCE, philosophers across the globe (both in the East and West) began to suggest that the good life was not simply about honor achieved through self-sacrifice on behalf of the community but was about learning the moral absolutes of the universe and then living your life accordingly. The framework for an identity

[1] *Here we are using "traditional" and "modern" as terms of time period as opposed to any value judgement. "Traditional" includes views held before the 1600s, while "modern" refers to views held beginning in the 1600s but which crystalized in the past century.*

was larger than just honor and included living a noble, good, pure life that aligned with the "Good" evident in the universe. A person should deny their base urges in favor of the higher desires of a moral life, seeking to become a thoroughly virtuous person.

Although this was a slight shift from ancient identities, this new framework was still an external identity. As a man or woman, your job was to learn the external moral values of your society and world (mainly through a study of tradition and religion), and then live according to those values so you could be deemed a "noble, honorable, good" person by the authoritative figures of your society. Your job in life was to accept the moral absolutes by which the universe ran, and then align yourself (even your contrary desires and urges) with this moral absolute.

Toward the end of the Renaissance period, the framework for identity within the Western world began shifting again. In the 1600s, discovering the moral absolutes which governed the universe were no longer found through tradition and religion but through science and reason. Your identity was secure when you used your intellect to discover how the world worked and then lived according to these natural laws. By the 1800s, with the rise of Romanticism, moral absolutes were believed to be found through the arts and emotion. In this school of thought, a person finds the universal Good and Beautiful hidden within the human heart through personal self-discovery, and then shares this good through artistic self-expression. Thus began the slow shift among affluent Westerners, who held political and religious power within their societies, from an external morality and identity towards an internal morality and identity—the shift from a traditional framework to a modern framework.

Charles Taylor summarizes this shift as such:

> *Thus by the turn of the eighteenth century, something recognizably*
> *like the modern self is in the process of constitution, at least*
> *among the social and spiritual elites of northwestern Europe and*
> *its American offshoots. It holds together, sometimes uneasily,*
> *two kinds of radical reflexivity and hence inwardness, both from*
> *the Augustinian heritage, forms of self-exploration and forms of*
> *self-control. There is the ground, respectively, of two important*
> *facets of the nascent modern individualism, that of self-responsible*
> *independence, on one hand, and that of recognized particularity,*
> *on the other. A third facet must also be mentioned. We might*
> *describe this as the individualism of personal commitment. ... No*
> *way of life is truly good, no matter how much it may be in line with*
> *nature, unless it is endorsed with the whole will. ... This three-*
> *sided individualism is central to the modern identity. It has helped*
> *to fix that sense of self which gives off the illusion of being anchored*
> *in our very being, perennial and independent of interpretation.*

By the turn of the twentieth century, the modern identity formation process had crystalized. In a modern framework, there are no moral absolutes, no universal virtues by which to determine what is good and how to live a good life. Instead, each person looks inside herself to find out what she believes is good and moral. What is "good" for one person might not be what is "good" for another.

This skepticism of meta-narrative and increasing dependence on a modern identity framework was accelerated by the failure of the Enlightenment era, as evidenced by the events of WWI, and then more importantly two decades later by the events of WWII—when the Holocaust and atomic bomb were perpetuated by so-called "enlightened Christian" Western nations. If the enlightened elites could use scientific advancements to create such horrific weapons of mass destruction and world leaders could send hundreds of thousands of their soldiers to their death in the name of "honor," then maybe these authority figures could no longer be trusted and maybe the virtues of society were simply tools to benefit the powerful and destroy the vulnerable.

Within this new modern framework, validation also must move inward. No longer does your community, village elders, or your philosophers and scientists determine what is good and whether you are living up to this definition of good; because with no common standards of good, there can also be no external validation. Instead validation must also come from within. You must determine what is good and whether you are living up to this standard of good. Once you have determined this, you externalize this identity, presenting it to the outside world and asking that your community "accept you for who you are."

Here begins the modern journey of "project self." In our modern framework, each person—who has the time and means to do so—works on themselves and creates their own sense of self and self-worth, seeking to build their own identity and brand in the eyes of the world through the accumulation of money, sex, or power. One person might seek fame and fortune, believing this to be the "good life." Another might seek success in their job or success in their sex life. Each person defines their own good and then works hard to achieve that good so they can feel valuable in their own eyes. The modern identity has moved from outward to inward, from duty to desire.

Deconstructing Cultural Identities

Now that we have an understanding of the history of identity formation, as Christians we need to deconstruct and evaluate the traditional and modern frameworks to see how these frameworks compare to the teachings of Jesus. What are the problems with culturally defined identities? What are the strengths and weaknesses of external and internal morality, and external and internal validation?

The first question these cultural frameworks seek to answer is *where does good/morality come from? How does someone know the good they are to live?* The traditional model answers that "good" comes from outside of a person and must either be discovered through communal practices, tradition, religion, science, or art. It is ultimately the external, larger culture that affirms this definition of good which you have been taught or discovered. There is one universal Good for all people which is upheld by the community. The modern framework, in contrast, believes that there is no universal good, and that good is defined by each person as they look inside themselves. The only one who can affirm this definition of good is each individual person.

In examining the answers to this first question, we run up against our first flaw in culturally defined frameworks. When a human being or a group of human beings are the determiners of good and evil, there is always inconsistency, hypocrisy, and bias. History has shown that humans are notorious for defining things that benefit them as "good," even if they damage other human beings. Likewise, humans might have "good intentions" but no follow through; or they may do a "good" thing externally, while having hatred and malice in their hearts. Cultural frameworks focus on "what it is right to do rather than on what it is good to be," and on how to live up to man-made standards while losing sight of anything greater in life to love, adore, or obey. This is a "cramped and truncated view of morality" (Taylor). In a traditional society, you love and obey the community elders, and in the modern identity, you love and adore the self. In both cases, we are loving and adoring other flawed human beings, like staring at our reflections in a pond.

The second question each cultural identity process seeks to answer is *who gets to validate you?* Who gets to say you are valuable and good? In a traditional framework, a person is validated by their community. In a modern framework, a person is, in theory, validated by himself. But as humans, we are by nature social creatures, so the reality is that even in a modern world, people create their own identity but then seek out other humans who will validate, affirm, and agree with this identity. It may not be the village elders or parents, but everyone is looking for a group of like-minded people who will validate their man-made identity.

Again, just as with the first question, whether internal or external, traditional and modern cultures are looking to other people to validate identities. But human beings are by nature fickle and flawed. A child might be born into an abusive household where she is rejected and devalued; or a child might be born into a privileged, self-indulgent home where anything she does is praised and lauded, even when they harm others or fail to follow through on obligations. In both scenarios, the human beings doing the validating are flawed, and the child's sense of self-worth is undermined. Even validation solely from yourself can vary from day to day depending on your emotional state and physical health. Human validation is unreliable.

Finally, every culture must answer the question *what happens to those who fall short of our standards?* In the traditional framework, an unvalidated (i.e. dishonorable) person is shunned from society and lives on the edges of community. In a modern framework, an unvalidated person (i.e. someone unsure of who they are) experiences isolation, self-loathing, and insecurity because they have no identity to present to the outside world. In both frameworks, this sense of being on the outside often causes people to work harder to achieve validation, creates a need to compete with those around them to prove their worthiness, and may even lead them to further isolation as they realize their efforts are getting them nowhere.

There is no sure and steady identity in a culturally-based identity. When those around you reject you or when you reject yourself, there is no higher being to validate and accept you; there is no one to empower you as you seek to change and adapt; and there is no one to declare that you still have worth even when you are failing miserably. In a culturally-based framework, we work tirelessly to present a valid identity to the outside world, hoping that this fragile identity will be accepted by others, while any type of criticism leads to further isolation and loss of self.

When Your Identity Fails

This lack of security and identity in the midst of isolation and failure can lead to increasing levels of shame. We fall short of our ideal selves, or the "ideal self" portrayed by society, and we feel guilt which turns into shame. As Fossum and Mason explain in their book Facing Shame, "While guilt is a painful feeling of regret and responsibility for one's actions, shame is a painful feeling about oneself as a person." In our world, we feel guilt for things that we have done, but we often live with shame for not only what we have done, but for sinful things said or done to us, both of which result in long-lasting painful feelings about ourselves. In this way, "chronic shame is to internalize a critical gaze" (Rudzena).

This ongoing sense of shame leads us, just like Adam and Eve, to hide ourselves behind the fig leaves of false identities. In our modern western world, our shame leads us to take on new personas that we believe are more culturally acceptable or to put on masks that will draw attention away from our brokenness and vulnerability. We hide behind these masks and take on identities built on our race, gender, sexuality, interests, accomplishments, connections, friends, families, or socio-economic status. Sometimes we even put on a mask that laughs at our shame and guilt, choosing to flaunt our darkest sins, pretending our perversions and addictions are part of who we are and completely acceptable.

And yet the result of hiding and parading is being unknown, insecure, and fearful. As Douglas Coupland explained, "Nobody believes the identities we've made for ourselves. I feel like everybody in the world is fake now, as though people had true cores once, but hacked them away and replaced them with something more attractive but also hollow." Likewise Alan Mann in his book *Atonement for a Sinless Society*, wrote:

> *The self has a sense that it is defective and has a basic flaw that ensures its unacceptability and rejection by those whom it loves. Shame thus contains a fear of abandonment, loss of love, and so loss of self. … To put it simply, if I know the story I am telling you is a "cover" story, then the most sensible thing to do is presume that the self-story you are narrating does not tell me who you really are either. The chronically-shamed live in the shadow of their cover story. The result is that shamed people are afraid to merge their lives, their personal stories, with others because of a fundamental lack of trust in relating.*

All of this hiding, insecurity, loneliness, and fear has produced a deeply broken society. As Brené Brown so rightly summarized, "We are the most in debt, medicated, obese, and addicted generation of adults in American History."

A Christian Framework for Identity

Clearly our culturally created identities—whether traditional or modern—produce insecurity and shame because they are based on the flawed human attempts to achieve good. And yet, for most of us, all we know about ourselves is what culture has taught us to think. We come to the Bible, hoping to find a more secure identity, and yet the words of Scripture clash with almost everything our culture teaches us consciously and subconsciously. As N.T. Wright explains in *Scripture and the Authority of God:*

> *The question 'Who am "I"?' can no longer be answered as easily as once it could. No longer 'the master of my fate, the captain of my soul', the individual looks within and discovers a seething ebb and flow of different impulses. Heisenberg's uncertainty principle, which boils down in popular discourse to saying that the very act of observing things changes the things you observe, works just as well, worryingly, when you look in the mirror. The Bible has a good deal to say about who we are as human beings, and/or as members of God's people, and/or as followers of Jesus—not least that we are made in God's image and called to be people in whom that image is being renewed. We thus find that to hold in our minds and hearts what the Bible says about who we are, and to do our best to live by that, clashes head on with our culture, which questions and challenges not only the Christian view of who we are, but all fixed and settled views of personal identity.*

So what is a Christian framework for identity? How do the teachings of the Bible compare to the teachings of our cultures—whether traditional or modern?

Good Defined by God

First, the Bible states that "Good" is defined by and derived from God. He is the ultimate Good in the universe. Nothing and no one is better than, higher than, or more holy and perfect than Him. Every concept we have of justice, righteousness, perfection, wisdom, and goodness is derived from His character and the way He created our world. This is why the Scriptures tell us that praises are always happening in heaven and on earth. The angels are always praising God because He is the ultimate beauty and good; they say to each other "holy, holy, holy is the Lord God Almighty" (Rev. 4:8). Likewise, the created world is always declaring God's praise-worthiness, His glory. "The heavens declare the glory of God, the skies proclaim the work of his hands" (Ps. 19:1).

God is both the source of Good and the One who declares other things "good." In the opening chapter of Genesis, God creates the world, names its created items, and then declares different things "good." It is God who gives each thing its identity and declares it "good" because it is fully itself—the "self" God created it to be. Likewise, Proverbs 3 and 8 record that God created wisdom and used it in creating the world. Every good thing is created by God for His purposes and only remains good as it is used accordingly. So although we can examine the world and see an order to how it was made, which might lead us toward wisdom and goodness, every created thing is not a source of good in and of itself, but merely a signpost pointing to the Creator of Good.

A virtuous life, according to the Bible, is aligning yourself with the laws of God and living according to His purposes. This outward, external "good" which can only be fully realized in God, becomes an internalized "good" when we invite the Holy Spirit to live inside of us and to write His laws upon our heart (Heb. 10:16). In his book *City of God*, Saint Augustine defined virtue as "rightly ordered love;" for it is not enough to simply love God, one must recognize God as the greatest good, the ultimate love. Augustine explains:

> *Now physical beauty, to be sure, is a good created by God, but it is a temporal good, very low in the scale of goods; and if it is loved in preference to God, the eternal, internal, and sempiternal Good, that love is as wrong as the miser's love for gold, with the abandonment of justice, though the fault is in the man, not in the gold. This is true of everything created; though it is good, it can be loved in the right way or in the wrong way—in the right way, that is, when the proper order is kept, in the wrong way when that order is upset (XV.22).*

Validity from God

Along with morality (i.e. the definition of good), validity, or the judgement of who is good, also comes from God. It is He who calls something or someone "good." Before sin entered the world, God created male and female and called them "good" (Gen. 1:28, 31). He then blessed them and gave them a purpose in life—to be His image-bearers (Gen. 1:26–28). This was the greatest blessing He could have given them, to be like Him. Adam and Eve's sense of self and self-worth came entirely from God.

After Adam and Eve sinned in the garden, seeking to know what good and evil was apart from God, they soon lost their sense of self-worth—hiding from God and blaming one another as they spiraled into shame. And yet, even in their brokenness, God did not abandon them. Instead, He promised to reconcile them to Himself (through the future Messiah) and to restore them to their former identity as perfect image-bearers (Gen. 3:15). This promise was fulfilled in the life, death, and resurrection of Jesus Christ. Through Jesus' perfect life, God is reconciling the world to Himself—not counting our sins against us but declaring us righteous in His sight because of Jesus' perfect goodness (2 Cor. 5:19). In Christ, God validates us and gives us an eternal security in His love and acceptance. (More on that below!)

Finally, in the Christian framework, those who "fail" are not excluded from the community. Instead, as Christians, we understand our communal identity as those who all should have been excluded on the basis of sin, but who instead are all included on the basis of Christ's righteousness. When we "fail" this leads to godly sorrow and repentance, which leads to a greater dependence on Christ and a greater love for God, both of which draw us further into the community of faith! (2 Cor. 7:10). Recognizing our dependence upon Christ's righteousness results in a stable and freeing identity because we are no longer dependent upon human or cultural recognition; we are living from approval, not for approval.

So if our Christian identity is based on God's definition of good and His validation of us, what is the identity that God gives to us as His followers?

Holy & Blameless

Apart from God, we are slaves to sin, children of wrath, and enemies to God (Eph. 2:3; Rom. 5:10). There is nothing we can do to remove our guilt or hide our sins. What we need is to be given a new holy, blameless, and righteous identity. This is why Paul writes:

> *Or do you not know that wrongdoers will not inherit the*
> *kingdom of God? Do not be deceived: Neither the sexually*
> *immoral nor idolaters nor adulterers nor men who have sex with*
> *men nor thieves nor the greedy nor drunkards nor slanderers*
> *nor swindlers will inherit the kingdom of God. And that is what*
> *some of you were. But you were washed, you were sanctified,*
> *you were justified in the name of the Lord Jesus Christ and by*
> *the Spirit of our God. (1 Cor. 6:9–11)*

Here Paul is talking about what theologians call *justification*—the process by which God makes us right in His sight, forgiving our sins and declaring us free from guilt.

Not only does God the Father justify us, declaring us righteous and blameless in His sight, but the Holy Spirit then sanctifies us and makes us holy. The Spirit washes us from our sins, and gives us a new spirit and heart that is alive to God and desires to obey Him. The Spirit makes us holy and teaches us how to live a holy life.

This process of sanctification is a life-long process of the Spirit washing away (Tit. 3:5) and burning away (Lk. 3:16) the broken, sinful parts of us—all the pride, masquerading, hate, greed, and shame that has entered our hearts as we have tried to create identities grounded in people and accomplishments other than God. At times, this work of the Spirit can feel painful because we are admitting our failures, bringing to light our dark sinful desires, and confessing our sins to others. But the work is worth it. In the process of sanctification, the Spirit is making us into the holy people He created us to be. He first declares us holy and good (justification), and then He makes us holy and good (sanctification).

Madeline L'Engle, in her book *A Circle of Quiet*, notices that just as the burning bush was aflame with the presence of God (Exod. 3) and not consumed, humans experience a burning sanctification by the Holy Spirit. She concludes that it is the burning, purifying work of the Spirit which makes us holy and our true selves:

> *[The bush] was alive with flame and was not consumed. Why? Isn't it because, as a bush, it was perfect? It was exactly as a bush is meant to be. A bush certainly doesn't have the opportunity for prideful and selfish choices, for self-destruction, that we human beings do. … The part of us that has to be burned away is something like the deadwood on the bush; it has to go, to be burned in the terrible fire of reality, until there is nothing left but … what we are meant to be.*

When we become who God created us to be, through the work of the Spirit, we see that His goodness is now reflected in a small way in the goodness that we too have become.

When we fully realize the beautiful truth of justification and the promise of sanctification, we can begin to live out of a stable, God-given identity. No longer are we plagued by guilt and shame, instead we can confess our sins knowing that, "God is faithful and just to forgive us our sins and purify us from all unrighteousness" (1 John 1:9). Instead of the worldly sorrow over sin that leads to guilt, shame, and death, we can have "godly sorrow [which] brings repentance that leads to salvation and leaves *no regret*" (2 Cor. 7:10). Knowing that we are now holy and blameless in God's sight, we can run into God's presence instead of hiding in fear. We can pray bold prayers knowing that God loves to answer the righteous. And we can lean into the sanctifying work of the Spirit, no matter how painful it may feel, because we know that He is working to make us into our true, holy selves.

Fully Known, Accepted, and Loved

Having declared us holy and blameless, God invites us into His presence to experience intimacy with Him. As holy people, we can now once again be in the presence of our holy God. But He doesn't leave us on the fringes of His kingdom or the outer courts of His presence. No! He declares each of us fully known, accepted, and loved by Him. Jesus invites us all the way into the throne room of God, declaring us children of God and co-heirs with Christ! Romans 8 reads:

> *For those who are led by the Spirit of God are the children of God. The Spirit you received does not make you slaves, so that you live in fear again; rather, the Spirit you received brought about your adoption to sonship. And by him we cry, "Abba, Father." The Spirit himself testifies with our spirit that we are God's children. Now if we are children, then we are heirs—heirs of God and co-heirs with Christ, if indeed we share in his sufferings in order that we may also share in his glory. (Rom. 8:14–17)*

And 1 John 3:1 exclaims, "See what great love the Father has lavished on us, that we should be called children of God! And that is what we are!"

This is the ultimate source of validation. The Creator God who knit us together in our mother's womb and who knows all of our days (both before and after Jesus), has now declared us His beloved children and welcomed us to share in the glories of His divine power and inheritance! This validation is better than the praise of any parent, any boss, or any community. The King of Kings and Lord of Lords has included you in His family and declared you His beloved child!

We might see ourselves as the prodigal son (Lk. 15), who has to earn his way into his father's graces and earn a seat at the table, but the exact opposite is true. The Father sees us while we are a long way off and makes a way, through Jesus, for us to enter His Kingdom. He then clothes us with His robes of righteousness, seals us with His Spirit, places His signet ring of sonship on our finger, and gladly sheds His sacrificial blood to welcome us home with celebration.

The praise, affirmation, and sense of belonging that you long for can be found in Him. He declares you holy, makes you holy, and fully accepts you into the Kingdom of God, throwing a huge party where everyone is cheering your arrival (Lk. 15:10).

This is why the Bible is full of marriage imagery. It's the only way God can explain the abundant love and delight He takes in His redeemed people. Isaiah 62:5b reads, "As a groom rejoices over his bride, so your God will rejoice over you." And Zephaniah 3:17 says, "The Lord your God is among you; He is mighty to save. He will rejoice over you with gladness; He will quiet you with His love; He will rejoice over you with singing." This is the way the Lord sees you and delights in you!

Divine Purpose & Calling

Not only are we holy and dearly loved, but God restores to us our divine purpose as human beings. When we seek to answer the questions *"who am I?"* and *"why am I here?"* we can confidently answer these as part of our new identity in Christ.

Jesus as the perfect Son of Man and perfect Second Adam (1 Cor. 15:45) reclaimed for humanity its calling to be image-bearers for God on earth. Out of this authority, Jesus invites us to be His image-bearers in our world, bringing the rule and reign of God wherever we go. Jesus sends us out to declare the gospel (the Great Commission) and to renew our world (the Cultural Mandate). Before His ascension, Jesus said, "All authority in heaven and on earth has been given to me. Therefore go and make disciples of all nations, baptizing them in the name of the Father and of the Son and of the Holy Spirit, and teaching them to obey everything I have commanded you. And surely I am with you always, to the very end of the age" (Matt. 28:18–20). When we ask the question *"what is my purpose on earth?"* we can confidently say that it is to make disciples and bring God's kingdom to every sector of society and every part of our world.

Not only are we given back the divine purpose of humanity, but we are also uniquely designed by God, "His handiwork/masterpiece," for specific "good works He has prepared in advance for us to do" (Eph. 2:10). As we follow the leading of the Holy Spirit, we begin to discover the spiritual gifts He has given to each of us to build up the church and advance His kingdom (1 Cor. 14:12); and we learn our unique callings in each season of life. As we grow in confidence in our new identities, we can confidently answer the question *"why am I here?"* and *"why am I here in this city?"*

A Christian Identity in a Modern World

Now that we know about our new identities in Christ, *how do we begin to live these out in the midst of a culture that seeks to form us in a different direction? Is a counter-cultural life possible in a city like ours?*

In John 17, Jesus prayed to the Father for his disciples, saying, "They are not of the world any more than I am of the world. My prayer is not that you take them out of the world but that you protect them from the evil one. They are not of the world, even as I am not of it. Sanctify them by the truth. As you sent me into the world, I have sent them into the world" (17:14b–18). Jesus did not intend to take His disciples, with their new identities, out of the world; instead He wanted them to be sent into the world to bring the good news. In order for them to remain in His love, and not be swayed by the culture around them, Jesus asked that God would protect them from the evil one and sanctify them by the truth.

Jesus' words are still true today. We are not meant to leave the modern world behind and escape into Christian enclaves; instead we are called to live in the world, while not being of the world. We can be people who live in and not of, as we are sanctified by the Spirit in truth and protected by God from the evil one.

Being sanctified by the Spirit, (i.e. being defined and shaped by Truth) is an ongoing process. Our modern world will still assign to us culturally shaped identities based on race, gender, sexuality, personality type, family, status, and industry. Our culture will still seek to send us through its identity formation process, telling us (directly and indirectly) that we must do certain things in order to be validated and act in certain ways to be accepted. Jesus told His disciples that, at times, the world might even label them as outcasts and dangerous because they were Christians (Matt. 10:22). And yet, in the midst of these pressures, we can still cling to the truth of God's Word.

Paul calls this process of clinging to God's truth in the midst of a culture of false identities, "putting off" and "putting on." "You were taught, with regard to your former way of life, to put off your old self, which is being corrupted by its deceitful desires; to be made new in the attitude of your minds; and to put on the new self, created to be like God in true righteousness and holiness" (Eph. 4:22–24). When the world tells us we are one thing, or that we should pursue certain desires and achievements, we are to take off this false sense of self. We are to renounce the lies that our sense of self and value is primarily defined by our achievements, others' approval, or other identity markers. After putting this off, we then choose to put on our true identities as beloved, holy children of God. We find our primary sense of self and value in our new God-given identity and consider all other identity markers (such as race, gender, industry, class) as far inferior to this first identity.

To return to Saint Augustine, living out of a God-given identity in a modern world is really about rightly ordered passions leading to a rightly ordered identity. We love God first and foremost, and so derive our primary identity from His love and approval. We see His purpose for our life as primary, and all other culturally-based purposes as secondary. You are a child of God first, and then a mother. You are a child of God first, and then an economist. You are a child of God first, and then Hispanic-American. You are a child of God first, and then a Democrat. All other secondary identity markers may come and go, or you might even "fail" at living up to them; but your primary identity as a child of God will never change.

This right ordering of identities then gives us integrity. Underneath all of the various hats we wear and societal roles we play, there is an underlying consistent identity. The hats of mother, economist, and Hispanic-American might come on and off depending on the season of life, but your identity in Christ remains unchanging. Beloved, holy, divinely-called child of God is your consistent, primary identity. This is the definition of integrity: to be one thing (from the mathematical term integer) in every situation in life. No matter the people we are with, the hardship we are facing, or the work we are doing, we are always the same person—a beloved child of God.

This integrity gives us, and those around us, the stability of character we long for. As Proverbs teaches, "Whoever walks in integrity walks securely" (10:9a) and "The integrity of the upright guides them" (11:3a). No longer are we tossed to and fro by cultural opinions or self-reflective evaluations. No longer are we putting on and off various identities in hopes that this mask will win us approval and help us feel good about ourselves. Instead, we can live securely out of our new identity given to us by God and can make confident decisions based on His love and guidance.

Our world is filled with broken, insecure, striving people, but God offers us a new way to live. He invites us to live a life that is not plagued by doubt but is full of confident faith; a life that is not rooted in insecurity, but is grounded in His love; a life that is not filled with attempts to be "good," but that is stunningly beautiful and holy. God is inviting us to leave behind our ordinary lives and live extra-ordinary lives. In Him we can live a life firmly grounded upon His supernatural love and filled with His power to do the works He has called us to do.

Growing in your Identity

No matter where we are on our faith journey, we all need to continue to lean into our new identity in Christ. Putting off the old identities of culture and putting on the new identity as a child of God is a daily process. Based on your initial self-evaluation in the Introduction, here are some practical next steps for growing in your Identity.

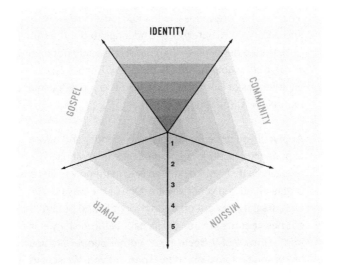

● **Know God's Plan:** If the ideas in this chapter are new to you, then the best place to start is by memorizing the Scriptures regarding your new identity in Jesus. Turn to Appendix A for a list of verses to meditate upon and memorize. Begin writing these out in your journal, saving them as images to your phone, hanging them in picture frames in your house, and meditating upon them daily and weekly. Learn to "hide God's word in your heart" so that when you are tempted to live out of culturally-defined identities, you can listen to the Spirit and live out of your new God-given identity (Ps. 119:11).

❷ **Experience:** If the ideas in this chapter are not new to you but you still struggle to believe that God sees you as holy, loved, and accepted, then this step is for you. Spend time in prayer this week asking the Lord to show you how He sees you. Set aside an hour of time in a semi-private environment to listen to worship music, pray, and read the Identity verses found in Appendix A. Tell one or two friends about this scheduled time and ask them to pray for you. During this time, freely confess sins, receive forgiveness, lean into God's love for you, and enter into His presence. God longs to put the truths of His Word deep inside your heart so you do not merely know it but whole-heartedly believe it. Record any experiences of God's profound love and presence in a journal for future reference.

❸ **Apply:** If you understand your new identity and have experienced God's love and presence on multiple occasions, then your next step is to learn how to live out of this identity in your daily life. One of the ways God encourages us to put off our old identity and put on our new identity is through His people ("iron sharpens iron" ~ Prov. 27:17). Begin inviting other people into your life to see the broken and holy parts of you. We suggest joining a C.O.R.E. group for confession, encouragement, and accountability in living out the truths of Scripture and sharing your faith with those around you. Let these people partner with the Spirit in His sanctification process, allowing them to speak into your life regarding sin, godliness, and your new fully-loved, fully-accepted identity in Christ. Oftentimes, other people have a clearer view of our transformation process than we do and can encourage us in the journey!

If a particular area of your new identity has been challenging to live out of, and if you find yourself repeating the same sin patterns, use the "Learning Circle" (see Chapter 1 of *Way of Jesus for the Renewal of the City*) to help you proclaim God's truth over that part of your identity, replacing lies with Scripture. Memorize any Scripture passages that are particularly relevant.

④ **Grow in Confidence:** As you grow in confidence in the love of God and the sanctification of the Spirit, begin learning how God uniquely created you. Discover your spiritual gifts and use them to build God's kingdom; chart out your life map to see God's calling upon your life; share your faith with those around you; and make strategic decisions to lean more into your unique calling and purpose in this city.

Self Reflection:
Ephesians 1

This week use T.I.M.E.,
described in the Introduction,
with Ephesians 1.

Ephesians 1:3–23 (NIV)

[3] *Praise be to the God and Father of our Lord Jesus Christ, who has blessed us in the heavenly realms with every spiritual blessing in Christ.* [4] *For he chose us in him before the creation of the world to be holy and blameless in his sight. In love* [5] *he predestined us for adoption to sonship through Jesus Christ, in accordance with his pleasure and will—* [6] *to the praise of his glorious grace, which he has freely given us in the One he loves.* [7] *In him we have redemption through his blood, the forgiveness of sins, in accordance with the riches of God's grace* [8] *that he lavished on us. With all wisdom and understanding,* [9] *he made known to us the mystery of his will according to his good pleasure, which he purposed in Christ,* [10] *to be put into effect when the times reach their fulfillment—to bring unity to all things in heaven and on earth under Christ.* [11] *In him we were also chosen, having been predestined according to the plan of him who works out everything in conformity with the purpose of his will,* [12] *in order that we, who were the first to put our hope in Christ, might be for the praise of his glory.* [13] *And you also were included in Christ when you heard the message of truth, the gospel of your salvation. When you believed, you were marked in him with a seal, the promised Holy Spirit,* [14] *who is a deposit guaranteeing our inheritance until the redemption of those who are God's possession—to the praise of his glory.* [15] *For this reason, ever since I heard about your faith in the Lord Jesus and your love for all God's people,* [16] *I have not stopped giving thanks for you, remembering you in my prayers.* [17] *I keep asking that the God of our Lord Jesus Christ, the glorious Father, may give you the Spirit of wisdom and revelation, so that you may know him better.* [18] *I pray that the eyes of your heart may be enlightened in order that you may know the hope to which he has called you, the riches of his glorious inheritance in his holy people,* [19] *and his incomparably great power for us who believe. That power is the same as the mighty strength* [20] *he exerted when he raised Christ from the dead and seated him at his right hand in the heavenly realms,* [21] *far above all rule and authority, power and dominion, and every name that is invoked, not only in the present age but also in the one to come.* [22] *And God placed all things under his feet and appointed him to be head over everything for the church,* [23] *which is his body, the fullness of him who fills everything in every way.*

Text

Read through the passage three times. Underline or highlight any words or phrases that jump out to you.

What does this passage mention about your identity in Christ? *(List those verses or phrases below.)*

Immerse

Choose two or three phrases or verses to study further. You might want to look up the definition for those words, find out where those Greek words are used elsewhere in the Scriptures, or study the theological and historical context for those verses. Write a summary of your findings below, and then choose one verse to memorize this week.

PHRASE A:

INSIGHT:

PHRASE B:

INSIGHT:

PHRASE C:

INSIGHT:

MEMORY VERSE:

Ministry

Now that you have read and studied the text, what is the
Spirit leading you to believe or do as a result? Why did the
Spirit highlight those phrases or words? What is He trying
to teach you about the gospel? How is He calling you to
live and act as a result?

Encounter

With all of this in mind, take this to God in prayer. Use the space below to write out a prayer and also to write out anything you hear God saying as a result. Then close your time by writing out a song/poem of praise to God.

MY PRAYER:

LISTENING:

MY SONG OF PRAISE:

03

Community

"The twentieth century will be remembered as an age of wondrous creativity, when Americans voluntarily shattered their lives into distant and dissonant fragments. America's industries learned how to assemble atomic bombs, airplanes, iPads and the genetic codes of life itself in the same era that American society disassembled the ancient overlap of family, food, faith and the field of work. Americans reached for the stars as they withered their roots, inhabited space but lost any sense of place."
— David Janzen

For many of us living in 21st century America, we prize our ability to choose and to express ourselves through our own personal preferences. The more affluent you are, the more you can personalize your world with flavors, colors, finishes, and services tailored to you. This has become so expected that we unconsciously carry these expectations into relationships. We may not be averse to commitment, but we certainly don't want to commit to something that runs contrary to our preference or limits our future choices. And yet all forms of community inevitably require a type of commitment in order to be vibrant and healthy.

Before we can dive into the rich topic of community, we need to look at how our culture thinks about commitment and preference, and how we've been trained to emotionally respond to commitment. Once we unpack these two layers, then we can compare this modus operandi with how God invites us into commitment with Him and others in the context of Christian community. It's in the midst of His God-designed community that we will actually find a better, freer, more joyful way to live.

A Post-Industrial Culture

Before the Industrial Revolution over 250 years ago, our world had been made up of agrarian, non-urban societies organized around long-term communities such as clans, tribes, extended families, trade guilds, or feudal land systems. Work and family were interlinked as large communities sought to survive off the land and labor together. This is the context of the communities in the Bible and of most communities up until the 1800s.

The Industrial Revolution changed much of this. Work was increasingly found in factories, outside of the home, and often in dense urban centers. Families became more and more dispersed as husbands, wives, sons, and daughters worked in different places and moved farther away from home to find new jobs.

The Industrial Revolution also changed the way communities functioned. Instead of a community being a highly interdependent family or farm, whose members all relied upon each other to survive, the value of the individual increased and the need for large communal thinking dissipated. Instead of a family being a large group that produced in order to survive, the family unit became increasingly smaller and more focused on earning income to consume goods outside of the home, as opposed to producing them within the home.

Over time, Western societies moved from industrial to post-industrial societies. In modern America, most of us no longer work on farms or even in factories; we work in office buildings in the service and information age industries. And just as the large communal system faded away in light of the Industrial Revolution, now even the smaller community and family units are vanishing in the wake of the post-Industrial Revolution. The individual is now primary. The concept of a "we" (as in a tribe or dynasty) has virtually disappeared, except in the form of teams shaped by workplaces designed to provide everything from lunch to laundry, so that as much of our lives as possible can be devoted to work.

The shrinking of the tribe to the two-parent household meant that instead of "thick communities," made up of a web of relationships based on lineage and survival, post-industrial society had instead "thin communities." As Aaron M. Renn explained in The Masculinist, "social activities whose decline in post-industrial America is now often bemoaned: the Kiwanis Club, the bowling league, the garden clubs, the labor unions, etc. These were thin communities that replaced the previous thick communities of extended family, guilds, monasteries, the feudal order, etc." And in our current post-industrial society, these "thin communities" are now replaced by what philosopher Zygmunt Bauman calls "peg communities" because they have no web of relationship, and instead are based upon the individual:

*Peg communities, Bauman writes, are communities forged by
disconnected spectators around a mutually loved experience
like a rock concert or a sporting match. Their participation
is a feeling or a sense around something shared. Ethical
communities, in stark contrast, are long-term commitments
that are marked by the giving up of rights and service.
In short, ethical communities are built on relationships
of responsibilities. These are relationships formed by
commitment, love, covenant, and even familial fidelity. One
of the fundamental shifts in our social matrix is that our
relationships are increasingly made up of peg communities
rather than ethical communities. (A.J. Swoboda summarizing
Bauman in* The Subversive Sabbath*)*

Instead of communities built on commitment, longevity,
and familial ties, our post-industrial society now has
communities built upon common interests and fueled
by shared experiences. We join a book club for a short
while because we want to read the newest mystery
novel, but as soon as the group picks a title we aren't
interested in reading, we leave the group. Or we attend
a Yankees game and feel bonded with the person sitting
next to us because we're cheering for the same team,
but if next week we sit next to a new stranger, we will
still feel the same "communal high" of the game, even
though we do not know that person's name or story.

Individual Preference

Over the past fifty years in particular, we as an American
people have been trained to value our preferences,
tastes, and freedoms above anything else. Selfies,
curated experiences, customizable drinks at Starbucks,
and Apple products fittingly called iPad and iPhone are
just a few ways we have learned to place ourselves, our

needs, and our desires at the center of our universes. We are taught to self-actualize and to experience self-fulfillment however feels "best for us."

In the 1970s, journalist Tom Wolfe Jr. dubbed the Baby Boomer generation the "Me generation" due to the rise in narcissism among younger generations. This similar critique was then leveled upon the Millennial generation when a 2013 Time Magazine article labeled them the "Me Me Me generation" due to a 58% increase in narcissistic personality disorder compared to those in the 1980s (as studied by the National Institute of Health). In essence, the "Me generation" (living towards the beginning of post-industrial America) gave birth to the "Me Me Me generation" (living firmly in a post-industrial society).

This focus in present-day America on the self and personal preference has only intensified our desire for peg communities instead of thick communities. A.J. Swoboda writes, "Today, in a world where we can find whole communities of people who think like us, share our values, and have common likes, we are trading in our ethical relationships for peg relationships. The result is troubling: We do not really need to love anybody who is different if we do not feel like it. We can cower in the corner with all the people we agree with."

Although preference and personalization are not inherently bad, they do lead to increased fracturing and isolation if we take our consumerism into our relationships. In modern America, we are increasingly sacrificing commitment-based community for thin, temporary human interactions based on personal preference. This choice is leading to instability, isolation, loss of freedom, and unknown identities.

Preference-Based Society

In a preference-based society people come and go based
on their current desires and emotions. There are few
long-standing relationships because everyone is self-
interested. As A.J. Swoboda writes, "In a peg community, I
am in so long as it benefits me. In ethical community, however, we willingly give ourselves to a community whether
it benefits us or not." In a preference-based society you
are in the book club as long as you enjoy the book being
read and you leave when you don't. There are no enduring
ties binding you to the people in the club which leads to
inherent, predictable instability in any group you join. Said
in a different way, "Where people no longer have the inner
daring to make serious promises or the grit to keep them,
human community becomes a combat zone of competing self-maximizers" (Lewis Smedes, "Controlling the
Unpredictable: The Power of Promising"). Everyone wants
their needs and desires met, so conflict ensues around
the decisions of the "group" and whose desires will win
out. Furthermore, we are less likely to keep agreements
if those past agreements no longer fit our present needs.
Preferences change often and, therefore, so do our "promises" since every company and individual is only looking
out for their own best interests. As Hosea 10:4 reads,
"They make many promises, take false oaths and make
agreements; therefore lawsuits spring up like poisonous
weeds in a plowed field."

A society focused on individual preference also becomes
increasingly isolated since there are no more abiding
"we" relationships. When individuals come and go from
groups where the members are forever changing, there
is no real "we" and individuals have no sense of belonging outside of themselves. BBC 4 Radio surveyed over
55,000 people ages 16+ in the United Kingdom and found

that "16–24-year-olds experience loneliness more often and more intensely than any other age group. 40% of respondents aged 16–24 reported feeling lonely often or very often, while only 29% of people aged 65–74 and 27% of people aged over 75 said the same." In short, those who were born before the post-industrial age experienced less loneliness—even though they were at an age in which many of their friends and family members would be dying or homebound—than those young people born into a post-industrial society who were healthy and mobile!

Surprisingly, another effect of preference-based modern culture is a loss of freedom. When we make decisions based solely on individual preferences we become increasingly controlled by our current emotions, bodily urges, and present thinking. Ironically while we are "free" to choose,, we actually lose our freedom to "fate" and "the mood of the day" which often keep us from carrying out our previous preference-driven choices and commitments. We do not exercise the freedom of control over our moods, bodies, or circumstances; we never rise above our mood or circumstances to proactively choose who we will be. Along with this, we also lose the ability to be a part of any group or community for an extended period of time, and, therefore, lose out on the freedom that comes from trust, intimacy, and growth over the long haul.

All three of these previous results—instability, loneliness, and loss of freedom—culminate in a fourth result: an unknown identity. In a preference-based society, I am what I currently feel and choose. There is no consistency around who I am and what I will do in the future. I am only known by my current actions and few people are around me long enough to even see these changes over time. Each room I enter, I am entirely new and only known by that day and that choice; and the same is true for each person I meet.

Commitment-Based Society

Let's now compare these four results of preference-based society with those of a commitment-based society: stability, intimacy, freedom, and identity.

In a commitment-based society, we can plan and make decisions based on our own and other people's promises. This creates an overall sense of stability since the future and relationships can be built upon these promises. As G.K. Chesterton explains, "On that single string—of a person bound to his promise—hangs everything from nuclear disarmament to a family reunion, from a successful revolution to a return ticket to Pasadena."

Lewis Smedes wrote a brilliant article 30 years ago entitled "Controlling the Unpredictable: The Power of Promising" which helps highlight the next three benefits of a commitment-based or promise-based society. He first explains that promising leads to greater levels of intimacy:

> *When you make a promise, you tie yourself to other persons by unseen fibers of loyalty. You agree to stick with people you are stuck with. When everything else tells them they can count on nothing, they can count on you. When they do not have the faintest notion of what in the world is going on around them, they will know that you are going to be there with them. You have created a small sanctuary of trust within the jungle of unpredictability: you have made a promise that you intend to keep.*

Each of us has experienced this result of promising when a friend showed up for us when we were sick, or when a parent continued to provide for us even when we were being a stubborn 3-year-old! When someone promises to be there for us, and then they are, this increases our trust, love, and respect for them.

Next, Smedes shows how making promises actually gives us greater freedom than when we choose purely based on our current preferences. It is our promises which allow us to rise above circumstances and fate, and choose:

> *Whenever a mere human being makes a promise, he stakes a claim on freedom. A promise is a momentous claim that the person who makes it has the power to act freely to bring order and dependability into the unpredictable future....We take it on ourselves to create our future with someone else no matter what fate or destiny may have in store. This is almost ultimate freedom.... The paradox of promising is that we freely bind ourselves to keep the promise we make. We limit our freedom so that we can be free to be there with someone in his future's unpredictable storms. 'The person who makes a vow,' said Chesterton, 'makes an appointment with himself at some distant time or place.'*

He goes on to explain that "a promise, then, is the human essence of freedom after the style of God—it is your freedom to be there with someone even though you cannot tell what 'being there' is going to be like for you." It is our promises which make us less like animals (who are predominantly controlled by their bodily and emotional functions) and more like the divine.

Finally, Smedes concludes that promises and our consistency in fulfilling them are what actually give us our identity: "We know someone as the same person today that he or she was yesterday by the promises that person made yesterday and keeps today....What I promise is what I am and will be to [my people, the ones who belong to me, who depend on me]...Promise making is the social bond that tells us who we are in our life together." You are a mother because you make and keep promises to provide for your children. You are a teacher because you make and keep promises to a classroom of students. You are not who you are based on what you wish to be but based on what you do each day consistently.

A Fear of Commitment

As our culture has shifted from pre-industrial to industrial to post-industrial, we have not only been trained to move from group-thinking to individual thinking, and from commitment-based decision making to preference-based decision making, but we have also witnessed an erosion of the central promises and covenants that used to give stability to our families and worlds. This secondary shift has had an impact not only upon our thinking but also upon our emotions.

Deep down, many of us living in postmodern America have a fear of commitment. This is not just because we do not want to limit our preferences, but because we are afraid that the person, people, and even God we commit to will abandon us and let us down. We are afraid to make commitments and promises because, even if we keep our side of the agreement, we are convinced there is a good chance the other person/party won't uphold their end of the bargain. And we fear this because we know deep down the instability of our own urges, which may keep us from being faithful to the promise. Having lost faith in ourselves and others, we avoid commitments.

For our post-industrial generation, much of this is rooted in our childhoods. When on average 50% of marriages now end in divorce (a large increase from the late 1800s) and the number of marriages per 1,000 adults has dropped by 30% in the past century, many adults living in America have come from divorced parents or have witnessed divorced relatives (Olson, "144 Years of Marriage"). If the first covenant commitment you witnessed as a child ended in heartbreak, then why would you believe in future commitments?

Our generation has also witnessed an increase in civil litigations over the past 30 years, corruption within law enforcement, political scandals (from Watergate to the Clinton impeachment hearings), and an increase in reported sexual assaults—often within the Catholic and Protestant church. If our legal, political, and religious organizations cannot uphold their oaths to the public, then why would you choose to commit to any group of people or authority figure?

Because the central promise-making figures in our life— our families and our government agencies—are unable to keep their promises, then we too have concluded that it is safer to live based on our individual preferences than based on communal commitments. We fear that if we commit to any person or group we might be limiting ourselves and will eventually become miserable. We also fear these people will ultimately abandon us, let us down, and take advantage of us.

The shrinking of the tribe to the individual, and the erosion of the central promises and covenants in our lives has encouraged us to become transient people who never stay in one place, one job, or one relationship for an extended period of time. This transience compounds upon itself as we avoid commitments because we "aren't here for long." Why commit if you aren't planning on staying, and why stay if you have no commitments to keep you there?

And yet, if we never commit to anyone or any community, then we face the risk of never experiencing the joy of lifelong intimacy, and the trust and stability that come from mutually committed relationships (like marriage and family). If we never move past temporary peg communities into longer-term commitment-based relationships, then we will be left with no one who truly knows us and can help us in our times of need. And finally, if we never commit to anyone, then we will never experience the truth that it is better to give than to receive, and the freedom that comes in serving others we are committed to.

Alfred Lord Tennyson famously said, "'tis better to have loved and lost than never to have loved at all." This is the dilemma of our post-industrial age. Will we risk love and possibly get hurt, or will we instead play it safe, and therefore never experience love and intimacy? C.S. Lewis summarized the risk of commitment quite poetically when he wrote:

> *To love at all is to be vulnerable. Love anything, and your heart will certainly be wrung and possibly be broken. If you want to make sure of keeping it intact, you must give your heart to no one, not even to an animal. Wrap it carefully round with hobbies and little luxuries; avoid all entanglements; lock it safe up in the casket or coffin of your selfishness. But in that casket—safe, dark, motionless, airless—it will change. It will not be broken; it will become unbreakable, impenetrable, irredeemable. The alternative to tragedy, or at least the risk of tragedy, is damnation. The only place outside Heaven where you can be perfectly safe from all the dangers and perturbations of love is Hell.*

The Way of Jesus

As followers of Jesus living in our preference-based, peg community world, we might be tempted to follow the customs and fear of our culture; to isolate ourselves in a "me and Jesus bubble," but this is not the way of Jesus. Instead, Jesus invites us to follow Him in His

promise-making and promise-keeping ways. God wants us
to risk it all for communal life with Him and His people.

A Promise-Keeping God

Even though God is the God of the whole universe and
could, therefore, do whatever He wants whenever He
wants to, He has actually chosen to live based on His
commitments instead of His current preferences. God
has chosen to be a God who makes promises in advance
and then keeps those promises, even if the person or
people He has made that commitment to lets Him down.
Every fear you have regarding commitment and abandon-
ment, God has faced head on and, yet, He still loves to
make and keep promises.

God not only makes promises verbally, but He formalizes
them through covenants (two-party ancient contracts).
Covenants were either between equal parties or unequal
parties (suzerain–vassal) and they were conditional or
unconditional. But every covenant always involved formal
promises—with blessings for keeping the promises and
curses for breaking them. A covenant also involved an
animal sacrifice (blood to represent the curse of covenant
breaking), a communal meal (to symbolize the new relationship), and then a sign (to remind both parties to keep
their promises). We see God enter into a number of these
covenants throughout the Bible with Noah, Abraham,
David, the Mosaic Covenant, and the New Covenant.

God could have simply promised things to people, but
instead He used formal covenants to emphasize His
commitment to them. God wanted His people to be able
to trust His character and the things that He promised
regarding the future. Hebrews 6:17–18 summarizes,

"Because God wanted to make the unchanging nature of his purpose very clear to the heirs of what was promised, he confirmed it with an oath. God did this so that, by two unchangeable things in which it is impossible for God to lie, we who have fled to take hold of the hope set before us may be greatly encouraged." We can boldly enter into a relationship with God because we know He is faithful. The Bible is a testament to the fact that God is loyal, even when His people are not loyal to Him. He is faithful even when those He loves are unfaithful to Him. And He refused to abandon those He made a covenant with, even after they all abandoned Him on the cross.

His Invitation

As we learn about God's character and plan, we can see that, through the Scriptures, God is offering us a new way to live. A life not based on self-interest, momentary preferences, and sinful urges, but a life lived out of a committed relationship with Him, one in which we obey Him and love Him because He first redeemed and loved us. This is why both Jeremiah 31:31–34 and Matthew 26:26–29 speak of a new covenant that God is offering to all people.

Each of us must decide for ourselves whether we will receive God's invitation. He is offering us a relationship with Himself, through Jesus, in which we will be forgiven of our sins, receive a new heart and spirit that longs to obey Him, and know Him intimately. We are then welcomed into His kingdom, His people, and His family. But this is a choice which requires leaving behind our personal autonomy and preference-based living, so we can enter into an everlasting committed relationship with God and His people.

In accepting Jesus' death on our behalf and receiving from Him new life, we are immediately entering into a covenant with God and with His people. Do you see yourself as in a covenant with God? When you received salvation, did you recognize yourself as now in a committed relationship with the God of the universe, which requires love, commitment, and obedience? (Luke 10:27) The Heidelberg Catechism states: "What is your only comfort in life and in death? That I am not my own, but belong—body and soul, in life and in death—to my faithful Savior, Jesus Christ." In receiving salvation and forgiveness from Jesus, we choose to leave behind our self-led lives, which lead to sin and isolation, and are choosing instead to be led by the Spirit of God. Our preferences become secondary to His good purposes for our lives and all our commitments come second to our first love, Jesus.

Likewise, this new covenant with God guarantees us a better future than any other preference-based living, or even human covenants, can give us. We are fully known, loved, and accepted. We have access into the throne room of God to bring before Him our petitions and requests; and we know that He is faithful in loving us, and working all things for the good of those who love him. All of the benefits of a commitment-based society are fully ours in Jesus: stability in His love, intimacy with the God of the universe, freedom to become who we were created to be, and a God-given glorious identity.

The People of God

We may think of ourselves as only in a covenant with God, but that's not how Jeremiah 31:31–34 describes the New Covenant, enacted through Jesus' blood. This is a communal covenant God is making with His redeemed people. When you and I enter into a covenant with God, we are now also in a committed forever relationship with God's people, His body, His bride, the Church. We do not live the Christian life alone, nor are we allowed to pick and choose who we want to be our brothers and sisters in this new family. We are called into a people as 1 Peter 2:10 says, "once you were not a people, but now you are a people." Or if we were to paraphrase this, "you used to be an assortment of individuals, each living your own lives, but now God has made you into a unified, interconnected people."

Many of the invitations Jesus made to His disciples were corporate invitations; they were invitations to communal salvation and shared responsibility. Jesus made this clear when He said, "A new command I give you: Love one another. As I have loved you, so you must love one another. By this everyone will know that you are my disciples, if you love one another." (John 13:34–35) As Jon Tyson noted in Sacred Roots, "When radical individualism overshadows our faith, we will only process Jesus' teachings and wrestle with Jesus' call to discipleship as individuals. But according to Jesus himself, such individualistic treatment misses the full experience of faith." A life of faith is a call to love and commit to one another.

We see this commitment to the people of God lived out clearly by the first followers of Jesus in the book of Acts. Acts 4:32 says that "all the believers were one in heart and mind"—that is a deep level of commitment and unity! And Acts 2:42–47 says:

> *They devoted themselves to the apostles' teaching and to fellowship, to the breaking of bread and to prayer....All the believers were together and had everything in common. They*

sold property and possessions to give to anyone who had need. Every day they continued to meet together in the temple courts. They broke bread in their homes and ate together with glad and sincere hearts.

This was a level of community that was deeper than even agrarian, tribal community. This was a diverse group of people coming together daily to live devoted, unified lives as followers of Jesus.

Holy Community

In today's culture, we have loose communal groups built upon identity markers and personal preference, which are fueled by shared experiences. But in the Kingdom of God, He uses an entirely different paradigm to create holy community. God brings people together from many different backgrounds and renames them "the people of God." He then gives them a shared purpose in the world to build His Kingdom. Instead of allowing people to endlessly run after their own preferences and desires in search of, or in defense of, their individual identity, He gives each person a part to play in His shared mission. Each person is a unique, yet interdependent, part of "the body of Christ."

The holy community God is building through His Spirit is not built upon individual identity markers but upon a shared new birth. Every person who becomes a disciple of Jesus is "born again" through the Spirit and given a new primary identity as a child of God. More important than your natural birth (with your gender, ethnicity, and generation) is your spiritual birth, which bonds you to every other Christian throughout space and time. Out of this new birth is a community based upon God and not the self, or even the pre-industrial family. As Henri Nouwen explains:

> *Community has little to do with mutual compatibility. Similarities in educational background, psychological make-up, or social status can bring us together, but they can never be the basis for community. Community is grounded in God, who calls us together, and not in the attractiveness of people to each other. There are many groups that have been formed to protect their own interests, to defend their own status, or to promote their own causes, but none of these is a Christian community. Instead of breaking through the walls of fear and creating new space for God, they close themselves to real or imaginary intruders. The mystery of community is precisely that it embraces all people, whatever their individual differences may be, and allows them to live together as brothers and sisters of Christ and sons and daughters of his heavenly Father.*

Not only is holy community built on God, but it is fueled by the power of the Holy Spirit. Instead of seeking out a shared experience that comes from being spectators at an event, or experiencing emotional highs through a shared accomplishment, the community of God is fueled by the Holy Spirit's power and love flowing through it. The glue that holds God's people together is the Spirit. This is why Jesus, right before His arrest, prayed:

> *My prayer is not for them alone. I pray also for those who will believe in me through their message, that all of them may be one, Father, just as you are in me and I am in you. May they also be in us so that the world may believe that you have sent me. I have given them the glory that you gave me, that they may be one as we are one—I in them and you in me—so that they may be brought to complete unity. Then the world will know that you sent me and have loved them even as you have loved me. (John 17:20–23)*

It is the Spirit that works to unite completely different people into one body and church; and He does this so that the Son and the Father might be glorified through the unexplainable, beautiful love God's people have for one another.

Challenges to Christian Community

So if God is working to build a holy community built upon His redemptive work and held together by His power and love, why is finding a healthy, vibrant Christian community so difficult? And why is committing to a church so rare in our culture?

To start with, we need to recognize the stages every one of us goes through when we seek to join a Christian community. Stages which, if not moved through fully, can often hinder the growth of holy, deep-rooted community. These four stages are: excitement, disillusionment, adjustment, and growth. We begin our journey by meeting new people and joining in new things, which gives most of us a natural adrenalin rush. But, over time, the glitter of new community and new people wears off as we start to see the brokenness in those around us. When we hit the disillusionment stage, many of us can become frustrated, anxious, and bitter. Our preference-based self-interested thinking starts to kick in and we wonder if sticking around is even worth it, or if we should just switch to a new small group or church. And yet, we must press through stage two if we are to ever reach adjustment and growth, thereby becoming an interdependent and integral part of the Body of Christ.

How can we press through our doubts and confusion? First, we can ask the Spirit to help us remember our own personal neediness and the deep love and forgiveness He poured out on us. We are no better than any other Christian. Sometimes a good look into the mirror of our own souls will quickly remind us of our own pride and flaws.

Second, we can ask the Spirit to help us see the community as He sees it—deeply loved and forgiven. This is His beloved people, His bride which He gave His very life for. As He gives us His eyes to see others, we will begin to be thankful for those men and women He has put into our life. As Dietrich Bonhoeffer explained,

> *If we do not give thanks daily for the Christian fellowship in which we have been placed, even where there is no great experience, no discoverable riches, but much weakness, small faith and difficulty: if on the contrary, we only keep complaining to God that everything is so paltry and petty, so far from what we expected, then we hinder God from letting our fellowship grow according to the measure and riches which are there for us all in Jesus Christ.*

Humility and thankfulness can go a long way in helping us move past disillusionment and into adjustment and growth. It's in adjustment that we realize that the church was not created for us, and our own needs and preferences, but was created for God's glory and the benefit of all of His people. It's here we make the necessary journey of leaving behind our personal preferences in favor of the needs of the people as a whole. To move through adjustment to growth we need to acknowledge our own selfish tendencies, which often place our own needs above the needs of others. In coming out of an individualistic culture, we can often find it challenging to consider others better than ourselves. And yet, Paul tells us in Philippians 2:1–4 that we must experience this deep heart change in order to commit to God's people:

> *Therefore, if you have any encouragement from being united with Christ, if any comfort from his love, if any common sharing in the*

> *Spirit, if any tenderness and compassion, then make my joy complete
> by being like-minded, having the same love, being one in spirit and of
> one mind. Do nothing out of selfish ambition or vain conceit. Rather,
> in humility value others above yourselves, not looking to your own
> interests but each of you to the interests of the others.*

And this is how we learn to grow into the Body of Christ—
with the foot working in unison with and for the benefit of
the hand, and vice versa. As Paul explains in Ephesians
4:15-16: "Instead, speaking the truth in love, we will in all
things grow up into Christ Himself, who is the head. From
Him the whole body is fitted and held together by every
supporting ligament. And as each individual part does its
work, the body grows and builds itself up in love."

Building Community

Once we have overcome the initial challenges to community, we begin the long, beautiful journey of partnering with
God's Spirit in building a holy community. Here at Church
of the City, we have found that building often requires the
four Ps: Priority, Practices, Proximity, and Permanence.

Priority

We must learn to seek first God's Kingdom, giving His
people priority in our life. As we mentioned earlier, our
new identity as a child of God must take priority over
all other earthly identities. Building God's Kingdom
and serving those around us must take priority over
meeting our own desires and preferences. Jesus' desire
that we be a united people—that we would be one as
He and the Father are one—must take priority over our
own desires to be right or invulnerable. Community can

be messy and full of conflict, so unity must become our priority in order for true reconciliation to occur.

Practices

The Holy Spirit also builds a holy community through shared practices, given by Him to us for our edification. These practices include: worshipping together, praying together, studying Scripture together, observing the Sabbath together, sharing meals, confessing to one another, and being a generous people who meet one another's needs. The early church lived these practices out well:

> *They devoted themselves to the apostles' teaching and to fellowship, to the breaking of bread and to prayer. Everyone was filled with awe at the many wonders and signs performed by the apostles. All the believers were together and had everything in common. They sold property and possessions to give to anyone who had need. Every day they continued to meet together in the temple courts. They broke bread in their homes and ate together with glad and sincere hearts, praising God and enjoying the favor of all the people. And the Lord added to their number daily those who were being saved.*
> *(Acts 2:42–47)*

Proximity

Proximity is also necessary if we are to build a healthy community. Paul writes, "Because we loved you so much, we were delighted to share with you not only the gospel of God but our lives as well" (1 Thes. 2:8). We need to adopt ways of life that allow us to live and work near other people in our community so we can have more interactions with one another than just two hours on Sunday. The Jewish community has been living out this holy habit for generations. As A.J. Swoboda explains, "For many Jews who opt to not drive on the Sabbath, it becomes a day to 'walk together,' to be alongside one another on their way to worship. Some Orthodox synagogues even have Eruv lines, boundaries within which Jewish families must settle to create a strong communal geography where rich relationships become a possibility." When we live or work in close proximity to each other, then we can create a beautiful web of relationships built upon daily interactions and meeting one another's needs. We can share meals, unload groceries, babysit children, visit the sick, and pray for each other in person. This type of community also becomes a witness to our neighbors and coworkers as they see this holy community in front of them!

Permanence

Finally, a holy community must also be a covenantal community. God makes a covenant with His people and He wants us to also form covenantal bonds with each other. A covenant is about a long-lasting, often permanent, relationship. At the heart of a covenant is the commitment to love one another through the ups and downs of life; to enter into permanent relationships based on a commitment to love, not on our own temporary whims and preferences. This is why the New Testament is full of the command to "love one another." "A new command I give you: Love one another. As I have loved you, so you must love one another. By this everyone will know you are my disciples by your love for one another" (John 13:34–35). "Now that you have purified yourselves by obeying the truth so that you have sincere love for each other, love one another deeply, from the heart." (1 Pet. 1:22) "Be devoted to one another in love. Honor one another above yourselves" (Rom. 12:10).

It is in our permanence that Christian community transforms from being a "peg community" based on the shared experience of attending a church service to becoming an "ethical community" built upon eternal, holy relationships.

Growing in your Identity

As we learned in this chapter, it can be a truly cross-cultural transition to move from living for yourself to living among the people of God. Based on your initial self-evaluation in the Introduction, here are some practical next steps for growing in your love and commitment to God's covenant people.

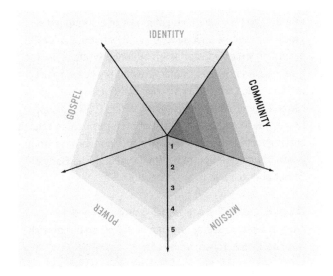

❶ **Know God's Plan:** If the ideas in this chapter are new to you, then the best place to start is by asking God to change your views of community. Deconstruct your views of community and compare these views with the Scriptures and topics shared in this chapter. How do they differ? Choose one or two verses regarding community to memorize and meditate upon. Begin attending a church regularly and ask God how He sees this church community.

❷ **Experience:** If the ideas in this chapter are not new to you, but you have never experienced covenant community before, then your next step is to join a community group (Bible study) and begin building relationships with other people in the church. Learn to see church as a thick (not thin or peg) community by getting to know people outside of Sundays in their daily lives. Invite other people into the various aspects of your life as well.

③ **Apply:** If you understand God's call to covenant community and have been a regular part of a community group for a while, choose to lean in further. Join a CORE group** in which you can learn intimacy, confession, forgiveness, and healthy conflict resolution. Learn to pray for, and place the needs of, your CORE group over your own personal preferences. Along with a CORE group, find a way to begin serving the church through an official serving team or opportunity with your community group. Learn to use your spiritual gifts to build up the Body of Christ and to serve those in need.

C.O.R.E. is a tool to use with 2–3 other believers to grow in Jesus together and can be found on our church website. The acronym stands for:

> **Confession** ~ Spend time reflecting upon your weeks and confessing to one another any sins so you can encourage and hold one another accountable.

> **Others** ~ Pray for anyone in each of your lives that does not know Jesus. Ask God to give you opportunities to share Jesus with them.

> **Read** ~ Share with each other what God is teaching you through the Bible.

> **Encourage** ~ Spend time encouraging one another

(not generically, but specifically). Exhort one another by "putting courage in" each other to continue to follow Jesus and grow in Him.

❹ **Grow in Confidence:** As you grow in confidence in serving and loving God's covenant people, begin reorienting your daily life and rhythms to be with the people of God and on mission with them. Reorienting your life will involve every part of your life—your living arrangement, career, finances, habits, prayers, weekends, and relationships (Think: priority, practice, proximity, and permanence).

Self Reflection:
1 Peter 1, 2

This week use T.I.M.E.,
described in the Introduction,
with 1 Peter 1 and 2.

1 Peter 1:22—2:10 (NIV)

²² Now that you have purified yourselves by obeying the truth so that you have sincere love for each other, love one another deeply, from the heart. ²³ For you have been born again, not of perishable seed, but of imperishable, through the living and enduring word of God. ²⁴ For, "All people are like grass, and all their glory is like the flowers of the field; the grass withers and the flowers fall, ²⁵ but the word of the Lord endures forever." And this is the word that was preached to you. ²ː¹ Therefore, rid yourselves of all malice and all deceit, hypocrisy, envy, and slander of every kind. ² Like newborn babies, crave pure spiritual milk, so that by it you may grow up in your salvation, ³ now that you have tasted that the Lord is good. ⁴ As you come to him, the living Stone—rejected by humans but chosen by God and precious to him— ⁵ you also, like living stones, are being built into a spiritual house to be a holy priesthood, offering spiritual sacrifices acceptable to God through Jesus Christ. ⁶ For in Scripture it says: "See, I lay a stone in Zion, a chosen and precious cornerstone, and the one who trusts in him will never be put to shame." ⁷ Now to you who believe, this stone is precious. But to those who do not believe, "The stone the builders rejected has become the cornerstone," ⁸ and, "A stone that causes people to stumble and a rock that makes them fall." They stumble because they disobey the message—which is also what they were destined for. ⁹ But you are a chosen people, a royal priesthood, a holy nation, God's special possession, that you may declare the praises of him who called you out of darkness into his wonderful light. ¹⁰ Once you were not a people, but now you are the people of God; once you had not received mercy, but now you have received mercy.

Text

Read through the above passage three times. Underline
or highlight any words or phrases that jump out to you.

What does this passage mention concerning God's
intention to form a covenant community?
(List those verses or phrases below.)

Immerse

Choose two or three phrases or verses to study further.
You might want to look up the definition for those words,
find out where those Greek words are used elsewhere
in the Scriptures, or study the theological and historical
context for those verses. Write a summary of your findings
below and then choose one verse to memorize this week.

PHRASE A:
INSIGHT:
PHRASE B:
INSIGHT:
PHRASE C:
INSIGHT:
MEMORY VERSE:

Ministry

Now that you have read and studied the text, what is the Spirit leading you to believe or do as a result? Why did the Spirit highlight those phrases or words? What is He trying to teach you about His people? How is He calling you to live and act as a result?

Encounter

With all of this in mind, take this to God in prayer. Use the space below to write out a prayer and also to write out anything you hear God saying as a result. Then close your time by writing out a song/poem of praise to God.

MY PRAYER:

LISTENING:

MY SONG OF PRAISE:

04

Mission

"Love is always giving itself away. When it is self-contained, it is not love."
— *Robert E Coleman*

Mission begins in the heart of God. God's mission, desire, and goal is for His kingdom to come on Earth as it is in Heaven. All of the earth will be like Heaven, "filled with the knowledge of the glory of the Lord as the waters cover the sea" (Hab. 2:14). This was God's good plan from the beginning—that every living thing and every human being would live in a good world and experience unhindered intimacy with God.

We talked extensively about the Kingdom of God in our first book, The Way of Jesus for the Renewal of the City, and also in Chapter 1 of this book. By way of refresher, God's kingdom is His rule and reign on the earth, and when God's kingdom comes, there is peace, righteousness and justice, joy, freedom for the captive, healing, and God's presence. God's mission is for Heaven to come to Earth so that His will will be done on Earth and every living thing will benefit.

In bringing His kingdom to Earth, God also intends to create a people to live in, benefit from, and co-rule over His earthly kingdom. God created humanity to be His image-bearers, and after the Fall, God's mission became to redeem humanity—rescuing us from sin, Satan, death, and Hell. Beginning with His promise to Eve, God sets in motion His plan to rescue a people for Himself and to reconcile to Himself all things through Jesus (Col. 1:20). When Jesus the Son finally comes to Earth, it is to fulfill the mission the Father has given Him: to proclaim the good news of the kingdom and "to seek and save the lost" (Luke 19:10).

Jesus knew that the kingdom of God—His rule and reign— would not be realized on earth until people who were far from God were brought near, having their hearts and minds transformed in such a way that they no longer live in rebellion to God but out of love and obedience. There could be no peace on Earth until humankind was remade from the inside out. The prophet Ezekiel spoke about this when he recorded these words from God:

> *I will sprinkle clean water on you, and you will be clean; I will cleanse you from all your impurities and from all your idols. I will give you a new heart and put a new spirit in you; I will remove from you your heart of stone and give you a heart of flesh. And I will put my Spirit in you and move you to follow my decrees and be careful to keep my laws. … you will be my people, and I will be your God. (Ezek. 36:25–28)*

Jesus came to bring God's kingdom by first redeeming and renewing humanity. Jesus satisfied God's perfect justice through His death on the cross, and then He sent His Holy Spirit to give His disciples a new spiritual birth so they would finally have hearts that wanted to obey God and live in His kingdom.

Jesus on Mission

Jesus' mission was fueled by love—a deep love for the Father and a deep love for fallen humanity. Romans 5:8 reads, "But God demonstrates His own love for us in this: while we were still sinners, Christ died for us." Mission begins in the heart of God because God's mission is fueled by and rooted in His love. John 3:16 reads, "For God so loved the world that He gave His only begotten Son ..." God loves the world and "wants all people to be saved and to come to a knowledge of the truth" (1 Tim. 2:3–4).

Jesus both demonstrated and taught about God's love for the lost. In Matthew 9:36–37, we read that "when he saw the crowds, he had compassion on them, because they were harassed and helpless, like sheep without a shepherd." We also see Jesus weeping over Jerusalem because the city was stubbornly refusing to accept His message of peace (Lk. 19:41–42). In parables, Jesus taught that God is like a shepherd who goes after the one sheep and then rejoices when He finds it, like a widow who searches the whole house for one lost coin and then invites her friends over to celebrate, and like a father who searches the horizon for his wayward son and then throws a huge party when the prodigal child returns home. This is God's profound love for humanity. Out of His love for us, God searches, finds, rescues, redeems, and restores humanity—transforming us from enemies of God to His beloved people.

Jesus stated that He came "to seek and to save the lost," and He accomplished this mission by praying, going, laying down His life, and then sending out His disciples to do the same (Lk. 19:10). Each morning, He woke up early to pray in an isolated place (Mk. 1:35). Before every major decision, Jesus went away and prayed, and He was led by and filled with the Spirit throughout His ministry. Jesus determined to only do what He saw the Father doing and to join Him in His work through the power of the Spirit, as one sent by the Father on His mission (John. 5:19).

Along with praying, Jesus went into the world to proclaim the good news of the kingdom, to teach the Scriptures, to heal the sick, to cast out demons, and to perform miracles. Everywhere He went, Jesus brought the kingdom of God with Him. He so embodied the Father's heart and will that He could confidently say to His disciples, "If you really know me, you will know my Father as well" (John. 14:7).

Finally, Jesus accomplished God's mission by laying down His life. He sought the lost, and He saved them through His perfect life, His sacrificial death, and His triumphant resurrection. And before His ascension, Jesus commissioned His disciples to do the same as He had done—to pray for God's kingdom to come and for workers in the harvest to go and make disciples of all nations, laying down their lives for others. We see this same strategy in Luke: "After this, the Lord appointed seventy others, and He sent them ahead of Him in pairs to every town and place where He Himself was about to go. He told them: 'The harvest is abundant, but the workers are few. Therefore, pray to the Lord of the harvest to send out workers into His harvest. Now go; I'm sending you out like lambs among wolves'" (Luke 10:1–3).

Jesus continues to live on mission through His disciples— even through His disciples in the twenty-first century. He invites us to live on mission with Him by praying, going, and laying down our lives for others. Jesus sends us out to the people, places, and positions He is already planning to go, freeing us to step out in courage, knowing that He will draw people to Himself as we faithfully pray and go.

Compelled by His Love

Just as Jesus was compelled by His love for the Father and His love for humanity, so we too are invited to be compelled by His love. Paul gives a concise theology of mission when he writes:

> For Christ's love compels us, because we are convinced that one died for all, and therefore all died. And he died for all, that those who live should no longer live for themselves but for him who died for them and was raised again. So from now on we regard no one from a worldly point of view. Though we once regarded Christ in this way, we do so no longer. Therefore, if anyone is in Christ, the new creation has come: The old has gone, the new is here! All this is from God, who reconciled us to himself through Christ and gave us the ministry that God was reconciling the world to himself in Christ, not counting people's sins against them. And he has committed to us the message of reconciliation. We are therefore Christ's ambassadors, as though God were making his appeal through us. (2 Cor. 5:14–21)

Here, Paul says that it is Christ's love for him and for the world which compels Paul to no longer live for himself but to live instead out of God's mission of reconciliation. Christ's love has transformed the way Paul sees the world and sees his life. Paul now sees his primary purpose as being Christ's ambassador.

For many of us, when we answer the questions *why am I here in NYC?*—we might say, "I'm here for work," "I'm here for family and friends," "I'm here for the culture," "I'm here

to make a name for myself," "I'm here to make money..."
If Paul were living in New York with us, he would answer,
"I'm here to be Christ's ambassador." This purpose state-
ment was certainly not true of Paul earlier in his life, when
he was seeking political and religious fame, but by the end
of his life, Paul is so full of love for others that he writes,
"I speak the truth in Christ—I am not lying, my conscience
confirms it through the Holy Spirit—I have great sorrow
and unceasing anguish in my heart. For I could wish that
I myself were cursed and cut off from Christ for the sake
of my people, those of my own race, the people of Israel"
(Rom. 9:1–3). Paul is compelled by Christ's love and burdened by God's deep love for the Jewish people and the
nations. Just as mission comes out of the depth of God's
heart, so Paul too is motivated to bring God's kingdom
from the depth of His transformed heart.

How did Paul undergo such a radical transformation? *How
is Jesus inviting us to be transformed in the same way?*
As we learn to live in the way of Jesus, Jesus teaches us to
seek new things, to see ourselves as sent, and to steward
our energies in a new direction. Together this transforms
our heart and life into one of mission.

Seeking the Kingdom

In Matthew 6:31–33, Jesus says to His disciples, "So do
not worry, saying, 'What shall we eat?' or 'What shall we
drink?' or 'What shall we wear?' For the pagans run after
all these things, and your heavenly Father knows that you
need them. But seek first his kingdom and his righteousness, and all these things will be given to you as well."

*What are you seeking first in your life? Why did you move
to NYC or choose to stay here?*

In this text, Jesus describes our propensity as humans to frantically run after many things in a panic. We chase after careers that we think will make us successful or secure; we chase after relationships that we think will help us feel loved; we chase after the approval we think will prove our value; we chase after better apartments, the latest fashions, the best deal in hopes of having financial stability. We worry and fret and seek after so many things!

But here Jesus is offering us a different way to live—a way of life that rests in the provision of the Father and seeks only the will of God. We take all of the energy that used to be directed towards worry and fear, and instead we use this energy to seek God's kingdom.

Instead of chasing temporary bread and temporary praise and temporary love, we are to seek out the eternal provision, praise, and love of God. We are to pray as Jesus told us: "Your kingdom come, your will be done on earth as it is in Heaven" (Matt. 6:10). We hope for God's peace, joy, and righteousness to enter our city; we pray that God's reign would be felt in palpable ways as captives are released, the poor are fed, and the sick are healed; and we long for God to renew our city through His people.

As you read these words, if you realize that your desires do not match God's and that you are not seeking first His kingdom, then ask for this burden. It truly is light. Jesus loves when we ask Him to help us and transform us.

A People Sent Out on Mission

Along with inviting us to seek the Kingdom, Jesus tells His disciples that He is sending them out to bring the

Kingdom to everyone. "'Peace be with you! As the Father has sent me, I am sending you.' And with that he breathed on them and said, 'Receive the Holy Spirit. If you forgive anyone's sins, their sins are forgiven; if you do not forgive them, they are not forgiven'" (Jn. 20:22–23). Just as the Father sent Jesus to earth to usher in the Kingdom of God and "to seek and save the lost," Jesus sends His disciples into the world to announce the good news of the kingdom and make kingdom-disciples. As Paul says in 2 Corinthians 5, "We are Christ's ambassadors"—people sent by the King to represent Him and His Kingdom to others.

But where are we sent? ... We are sent to people, places, and positions.

People

Often times God will send us to a particular group of people. For example, the apostle Paul was sent to the Greek-speaking world, Philip was sent, first, to an Ethiopian eunuch and then to Samaritans, Peter was sent to the household of Cornelius, and so on. Throughout history, men and women have been sent by God to specific groups of people, whether from their own culture or from another. And, as we discussed in The Way of Jesus, the gospel often spreads by people being sent into their families and local communities first.

Places

In His great commission, Jesus told His disciples that they would be His witnesses in Jerusalem, Judea, Samaria, and to the ends of the earth (Acts 1:8). With this in mind, the apostles went and sent their own disciples to cities and countries all over the world. Church tradition teaches that Andrew went to places north of the Black Sea, Thomas traveled east to Syria and India, and Philip journeyed south to North Africa. But while Paul was sent to travel all over the Greek-speaking world, Peter and James were sent to their own Jewish people living in Israel. Throughout Church history, men and women have been sent to far off places to bring the gospel, and they have also been commissioned by God to bring the gospel into their own neighborhoods and cities.

When we choose to follow the example of Paul, a forerunner for cross-cultural ministry, then we can learn to bring the gospel to people, both near and far, who are similar to us and to those that differ from us. Paul wrote:

> *Though I am free and belong to no one, I have made myself a slave to everyone, to win as many as possible. To the Jews I became like a Jew, to win the Jews. To those under the law I became like one under the law (though I myself am not under the law), so as to win those under the law. To those not having the law I became like one not having the law (though I am not free from God's law but am under Christ's law), so as to win those not having the law. To the weak I became weak, to win the weak. I have become all things to all people so that by all possible means I might save some. I do all this for the sake of the gospel, that I may share in its blessings. (1 Cor. 9:19–23)*

When we take the posture of a servant, we are willing to leave behind our particular culture and preferences in order to bring the gospel message into any culture or circumstance with respect for the flourishing of that culture and place.

Positions

The Bible also gives examples of people being sent into specific positions of influence or within specific industries. Paul served as a tentmaker for many years, shared the gospel in prison, and later appeared before foreign leaders—even Caesar! God blessed other disciples with the financial means to host churches in their homes, and still others with positions of authority within local government. William Wilberforce is a modern example of a man who was placed by God into British Parliament so that he, and others, could overturn the British slave trade and usher in God's freedom.

In the language of the Scriptures, all disciples of Jesus are sent to someone and someplace. Jesus does not appoint some to be missionaries and others to "sit on the bench." Jesus sends all who follow Him out into the world to proclaim the gospel and bring His kingdom. Michael Frost explains:

> *Sentness is not just for missionaries to foreign lands. The shift is for all of us—students and workers, parents and kids, professionals and laborers, artists and accountants, moms and mechanics. We are all sent into our world. We are given to those we relate to. We are commissioned to our workplace. We are placed in our streets. When our imaginations grasp our sentness, our life stories take on a whole new, dangerous meaning. As G. A. Studdert Kennedy has said, "Nobody worries about Christ as long as he can be kept shut up in churches.... But there is always trouble if you try and let him out." Jesus is not made for staying in churches, and neither are we.*

How could seeing yourself as sent change the way you view your life right now? What people, place, or position is Jesus sending you to right now?

Being sent as Christ's ambassador will not always be grandiose and monumental in the moment. Often times being sent means being Jesus' hands and feet in daily, small, faithful ways: praying for a coworker, babysitting a neighbor's children, working tirelessly to bring change in your industry, or learning a new language to share the gospel with a friend in their first ("heart") language.

While Jesus was on earth, He was confined to one tiny region, and His daily life consisted of feeding the hungry, healing the sick, and preaching the gospel to that small Jewish people group. And yet, His life and ministry shaped all of human history! This is why Jesus compared the kingdom of God to a small bit of yeast or a tiny mustard seed. Small acts done through the power of God's Spirit have disproportionate effects for the Kingdom. As Neil Cole writes, "Why is small so big? Small does not cost a lot. Small is easy to reproduce. Small is more easily changed and exchanged. Small is mobile. Small is harder to stop. Small is intimate. Small is simple. Small infiltrates easier. Small is something people think they can do. Big doesn't do any of these things. We can change the world more quickly by becoming much smaller."

Jesus is sending us, small men and women, out into our big diverse city to have disproportionate influence on the people, places, and industries that He wants to redeem and restore.

But how is Jesus sending us out? He sends us out praying and going, just as He did.

Praying

First, Jesus invites us to live on mission by praying—praying for workers and praying for the Spirit to move. In Luke 10:2,

Jesus instructs his disciples, "The harvest is plentiful, but the workers are few. Ask the Lord of the harvest, therefore, to send out workers into his harvest field." This is first a prayer of awareness, of lifting up your eyes to see the harvest, to see those around you who need the gospel; it means stepping out of yourself and your own concerns to be aware of the needs of others and begin interceding for them. Second, it's a prayer of faith, believing Jesus' words that the harvest of souls is plentiful, even when it doesn't look like it, and that the main issue is not the readiness of the harvest but the number of workers harvesting. Third, this is a prayer of release. When we ask the Lord to harvest however and whenever He wants to, we are releasing the results of the harvest into His hands. Finally, this is a prayer of readiness, knowing that God might call upon you to proclaim His kingdom at any time. But when you faithfully pray this prayer, you will be ready. In praying for the lost you have joined in God's heart, and a new desire has been birthed in you to see friends and neighbors saved. So when God asks, "Whom shall I send?" you will reply, "Here I am. Send me" (Isaiah 6:8).

Going

Just like Jesus did, as we pray, we are also sent out to go. Beverly James defined going while praying as, "Talking to God about our neighbors before we talk to our neighbors about God." And the root of this strategy is knowing WHO is sending us out—that He is the one who draws people to Himself. Jesus makes this clear in Matthew 28:18–20: "All authority in heaven and on earth has been given to me. Therefore go and make disciples of all nations, baptizing them in the name of the Father and of the Son and of the Holy Spirit, and teaching them to obey everything I have commanded you. And surely I am with you always, to the every end of the age." He has the authority, He sends us out, and He is with us, confirming the message we are bringing with His signs and wonders.

In Luke 10, Jesus also explains to us what we are to do when we go. First, we pray a blessing over any place we enter and person we encounter. "When you enter a house, first say, 'Peace to this house.' If someone who promotes peace is there, your peace will rest on them; if not, it will return to you" (Lk. 10:5-6). We are to ask God to bless this person and to change the spiritual climate so He can heal this place and this person and bring His peace into their lives. We see Paul employ this same strategy when he travels to new cities, asking others to pray for him before he goes, that a door would be open to the gospel (Col. 4:3).

By beginning with a prayer of blessing, God moves and softens our hearts so that we enter into a new place with joy, kindness, and thoughtfulness. This leads us to Jesus' second command: to eat with those we meet, having a posture of receiving. "Stay there, eating and drinking whatever they give you, for the worker deserves his wages. Do not move around from house to house. When you enter a town and are welcomed, eat what is offered to you" (Lk. 10:7-8). Eating with other people can be a powerful way to connect with others and enter into a relationship of mutuality—of giving and receiving. Jesus was quick to eat with others—Zacchaeus, the Pharisees, Peter, Mary, Martha, and Lazarus—and to say yes to an invitation to eat in someone's home. We too can imitate Jesus by saying yes when others welcome us into their life. And as we enter their life and share a meal, we can pray that the Lord would make us a sweet aroma (2 Cor. 2:25).

As we begin to enter another person's life, Jesus then instructs us to meet their felt needs with God's power: "Heal the sick who are there" (Lk. 10:9a). Jesus empowered His disciples through the Holy Spirit to confirm His message with signs and wonders, and meeting people's felt needs—whether by healing the sick or feeding the hungry—would serve as a tangible sign that God's kingdom had arrived. We too can ask the Lord to move in ways that are undeniable so that people's hearts are open to the gospel message. This was a central part of Paul's ministry: "My message and my preaching were not with wise and persuasive words, but with demonstrations of the Spirit's power, so that your faith might not rest on human wisdom, but on God's power" (1 Cor. 2:4–5). Jesus wants us to ask Him to pour out His power, which is why He promised us that we would do even greater works than He did (Jn. 14:12). He has all authority, and He has promised that signs and wonders would accompany the preaching of His gospel, so we need to cry out for Him to move! As Ed Silvoso explains in his book Prayer Evangelism, "Pray for miracles that meet the felt needs of unbelieving people. ... Prayer becomes evangelism when it's used to open the eyes of unbelievers to the divinity of Jesus." When someone sees God move in power to meet their needs or answer their prayers or questions, they are more receptive to learn about Him. As you serve them as an agent of God's love, they are more open to hearing from you about the specifics of God's love!

Finally, when we go, we are to proclaim the good news of Jesus, bringing the kingdom wherever we go and making disciples. As Jesus commands in Luke 10:9, "Heal the sick who are there and tell them, 'The kingdom of God has come near to you.'" The gospel is "the good news that God our Father, the Creator, out of His great love for us, has come to rescue us from sin, Satan, death and Hell, and to renew all things, in and through the work of Jesus Christ on our behalf, to establish His kingdom, through His people, in the power of the Holy Spirit. This is for God's great glory, and our profound joy." The Bible is clear that people everywhere are lost and dead in their sins, but that they can experience resurrection through Jesus. But as Paul eloquently puts it, "How can they believe in the One of whom they have not heard? And how can they hear without someone to preach?" (Rom. 10:14b). Men, women, and children across our city need to hear the good news of Jesus so they can respond to His Spirit and be saved. Jesus is sending each of us out into the harvest to clearly proclaim that good news to them.

Making Disciples

Being sent into the harvest not only involves proclaiming the gospel, but also teaching people how to follow Jesus and sending them out into the world on mission, just as Jesus sent you out. Before He ascended into Heaven, Jesus gave this commission to His disciples: "All authority in heaven and on earth has been given to me. Therefore go and make disciples of all nations, baptizing them in the name of the Father and of the Son and of the Holy Spirit, and teaching them to obey everything I have commanded you. And surely I am with you always, to the very end of the age" (Matt. 28:18–20). Jesus wanted His disciples to make more disciples who would make more disciples, so that eventually everyone in the world would have the chance to hear the good news concerning Jesus Christ.

In his insightful book *The Master Plan of Evangelism*, Robert E. Coleman describes Jesus' mission to not only bring salvation to a few hundred people living in first-century Israel, but to bring salvation and whole-life transformation (i.e. sanctification) to the ends of the earth through reproducing disciples. Jesus followed these eight steps and taught His disciples to do likewise: select teachable people to be His disciples, remain in close association and relationship with them, consecrate these people for the mission, impart His teachings and way of life to them, demonstrate how to daily live out of a Kingdom paradigm, delegate to them to begin sharing the gospel, supervise them as they continue to grow, and then show them how to produce multiplying disciples themselves. This was Jesus' method for teaching people how to become His disciples and then make new disciples.

Jesus' desire then and now is that everyone would hear the good news of God's kingdom *(evangelism)*, that men and women would experience salvation and a new birth through the renewing work of the Holy Spirit *(salvation)*, that these men and women would then be taught by the Spirit through other believers how to wholeheartedly follow and obey Jesus *(sanctification)*, and that these new disciples would then go out into the world proclaiming the good news, bringing the Kingdom, and making disciples of other people *(missional disciples)*.

Stewardship

By inviting us to seek first God's kingdom, Jesus is not only inviting us to orient our lives in a certain direction and to be sent to specific people or places, but He is also inviting us to steward all of our energies in that direction as well. As Paul wrote in 2 Corinthians 5, "He died for all, that those who live should no longer live for themselves but for him." Just as Jesus laid down His life, we are invited to also lay down our lives for God's mission—no longer living for our own mission but for God's.

How are you allocating your life? What are you putting your energy toward to build and amass?

In our culture, we are encouraged to pursue personal ambitions, to work on "project self," and to pursue our best life. We tend to steward our energies in this order: financial wealth and stability, physical vitality and pleasure, and intellectual pursuits, accomplishments, and expertise. Then we want our relational needs met through friends or family that help us reach our personal goals. And finally, we might sprinkle in some spiritual interests to buoy our emotions.

And yet, when we seek first God's kingdom, this list of priorities gets rearranged and our energies are reallocated. We begin with the spiritual, seeking God first; then we put energy toward the relational as we lay our lives down for others and invite them into God's kingdom; we then offer our physical bodies as a living sacrifice to God's mission, and with this we also offer our mind and our resources to be used to advance His kingdom. Our lives are now marked by worship, love, servanthood, and generosity. As David Nagel explains, "One of the primary purposes of the gospel is the reordering of our deepest loves and affections. It gives us new purposes and desires for our lives in this world, here and now. Reordered love implanted in a transformed heart is the distinctive mark of the Christian."

Building God's kingdom involves stewarding our energies towards kingdom values and practices in everything we do. As we mentioned in Chapter 1, the prophet Isaiah gives a vivid picture of life in God's kingdom which includes salvation, righteousness and justice, peace, joy, God's presence, healing, and a return from exile. What would it look like if you actively stewarded your resources toward building God's kingdom in this city? How might you steward your time and energy toward actively sharing the gospel with your neighbors so salvation could come to your block? What would it look like to actively seek peace and wholeness in your relationships? How might you work toward freeing the enslaved and oppressed in your industry? How could you spend your early mornings ushering in the presence of God through prayer and worship? How might you give your money and free time toward justice initiatives in our city?

Living on Mission

As we can see, Jesus is inviting us into an entirely new way of living—to seek His kingdom first, to see ourselves as sent people, and to steward all of our resources and energies toward building His kingdom. This new way of life—of living on mission—has a particularly profound effect on New Yorkers.

New York teaches us to live on mission for ourselves—to be ambitious and build project self. But soon, all of our dreams for life in New York begin to fade because we either don't achieve what we want or we are disappointed when we do achieve our goals. So instead of ambition, we learn to say "this will do for now." As the pressure of New York builds, our lack of personal satisfaction and fulfillment becomes "this will have to do." Finally as stress increases, rent increases, etc., we think "this won't do" and we leave the city.

But Jesus invites us to not begin with Personal Ambition but with God's Mission. In this alternate timeline, we come to New York because we were sent. When life is challenging, we turn to God in prayer, asking Him to provide for our needs, to sustain us with His daily bread, and to fill us with His power. So sentness leads to healthy dependence. Out of dependence comes empowerment, as we learn to be filled with the power and resources of God's Spirit. And out of dependence and empowerment, flow the fruits of the Spirit and the signs of the kingdom. We become a fruitful people, seeing people drawn into God's kingdom. And out of fruitfulness, comes joy and contentment. Like Paul, we can say, "I have learned to be content whatever the circumstances. I know what it is to be in need, and I know what it is to have plenty. I have learned the secret of being content in any and every situation, whether well fed or hungry, whether living in plenty or in want. I can do all this through him who gives me strength" (Phil. 4:11–13).

When we choose to live out of God's mission instead of our own personal ambition, Jesus makes us this beautiful promise: "Seek first the kingdom and His righteousness, and all these things will be added to you as well" (Matt. 6:3). When we pour ourselves out for God's plans, we paradoxically receive back from God the security, love, resources, and significance we were originally tempted to run after. There are times when obeying God might entail sacrifice and suffering (as we see in the lives of Jesus and His disciples); but we can face these trails, like the disciples and Jesus, who for the joy set before them counted their suffering all as loss for the sake of knowing Jesus and receiving an eternal weight of glory (Heb. 12:2, Phil. 3:8–10, 2 Cor. 4:17). In the end, God gives us all of the love, joy, and glory our hearts are longing for.

As you look at these two storylines, these two ways of living: *How would your life change if you saw yourself on Mission here in the city … not on a mission to meet your own needs or accomplish your own plans, but on mission to seek and bring the kingdom to New York?* What if the words of 2 Corinthians 5 became true in your life? What if you felt compelled by Christ's magnificent love to live not

for yourself but for Him, so that through your radical aban-
donment, God could make His appeal to those around you,
reconciling them to Himself?

And what if you weren't alone in this mission? Imagine
what our city would be like if a group of people lived
whole-heartedly, fully "sold out" for the mission of God—
—seeking first His kingdom, seeing themselves as sent
out to bring in His kingdom, and stewarding all of their
resources in that direction.

We have seen beautiful examples of this in our church as
community groups gather to serve the poor and homeless
in our city, to welcome in the handicapped and mentally
challenged, and cook delicious meals for coworkers while
exploring faith through the Alpha course. Men and women
have generously given of their time, talents, and finances
to meet the needs of others, launch new ministries, and
build a 24/7 prayer room here in New York. Together we
have begun to plant the seeds of revival in our city, believing that God wants to bring His kingdom here in New York
as it is in Heaven.

Contending for His Promises

God's deepest desire is to reconcile all things in Heaven
and Earth to Himself (Col. 1), and He invites us to be
a part of this glorious work. He invites us to live on
mission and contend with Him for His promises. Just
as Abraham contended with God to rescue Sodom and
Gomorrah, Jacob wrestled with God for blessing, and
Moses pleaded with God to remain with the people of
Israel, so too God wants us to pray His promises into
being (Gen. 18, Gen. 32, Exod. 33).

Contending for God's promises involves taking the promises of God written in the Scriptures and praying them back to Him, asking Him to fulfill His promise to these people, in this place, in this time. We see the prophet Habakkuk demonstrate this when he prays, "Lord, I have heard of your fame; I stand in awe of your deeds, Lord. Repeat them in our day, in our time make them known; in wrath remember mercy" (Hab. 3:2).

As we pray for God to pour out His Spirit in our generation, God often gives us a specific burden related to the people, places, and positions to which He has sent us. This is a special God-given yearning, as if we carry a small part of His heart for our broken world. It's out of this God-given burden that we pray with passion and confidence. We learn to carry God's longing for these people and bring this longing before His throne of grace, moving into the position of the intercessor. Like Jesus, we become the holy priests interceding for these people before our Holy God. And this is a beautiful thing, because God has called us to be a "royal priesthood" (1 Pet. 2:9).

As we cry out for God to fulfill His mission in our city and our generation, we will see God move in response to the prayers of His people. As the apostle John explains, "This is the confidence we have in approaching God: that if we ask anything according to his will, he hears us. And if we know that he hears us—whatever we ask—we know that we have what we asked of him" (1 Jn. 5:14–15). Jesus wants us to pray His promises into being. As Walter Wink explains, "Intercessory prayer is spiritual defiance of what is in the way of what God has promised. Intercession visualizes an alternative future to the one apparently fated by the momentum of current forces. Prayer infuses the air of a time yet to be into the suffocating atmosphere of the present. History belongs to the intercessors who believe the future into being."

May we go out in the power of the Spirit, compelled by Christ's love, and become intercessors fueled by a holy imagination who believe God's glorious future into being.

Growing in your Identity

As we learned in this chapter, God intends for all of His disciples—each and every person—to live on mission. Based on your initial self-evaluation in the Introduction, here are some practical next steps for growing in your love and commitment to God's covenant people.

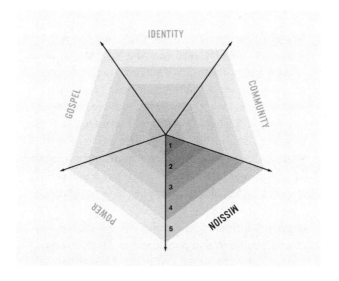

● **Know God's Plan:** If the ideas in this chapter were new to you, then the best place to start is by asking God to change your views of your own purpose and calling. Begin meditating and memorizing your new identity as Christ's ambassador. Ask the Lord to show you where and to whom He has already sent you. Begin learning about God's kingdom and His heart for our world. Let His desires for redemption and renewal change your thinking.

● **Experience:** Once you have asked the Lord to show you where and to whom He may have already sent you, go into that place and to that people asking Him for an opportunity to share the gospel and/or bring in kingdom values. Ask the Spirit to fill you with His love and wisdom, preparing your heart and their heart for this God-ordained moment. Prayerfully step out in faith as the Holy Spirit leads you. Afterwards, record what happened in a journal and "debrief" with God. Commit to praying for this person or place.

3. **Apply:** As you begin to know where God has sent you, reallocate your time, energy, and emotions around seeking and bringing God's kingdom to that place, position, or people. Intentionally build missional relationships, look for daily ways to serve and love others, and start giving your time and energy to God's kingdom. Ask the Spirit to empower you to be His ambassador. Write out a three-minute and ten-minute version of your testimony (how Jesus rescued and changed you) to share with others [See Appendix C].

4. **Grow in Confidence:** Go with confidence to the places, positions, and people groups God has sent you to. Steward your gifts, intellect, finances, etc. in this direction, and continue to pursue opportunities to develop these gifts and skills. Spend extended times in prayer for these people, places, and industries. Pray boldly, knowing that God Himself has sent you to these people as His ambassador, so He wants to hear and answer your prayers.

Self Reflection:
Luke 10

This week use T.I.M.E.,
described in the Introduction,
with Luke 10.

Luke 10:1–12, 17–24 (NIV)

¹*After this the Lord appointed seventy-two others and sent them two by two ahead of him to every town and place where he was about to go.* ² *He told them, "The harvest is plentiful, but the workers are few. Ask the Lord of the harvest, therefore, to send out workers into his harvest field.* ³ *Go! I am sending you out like lambs among wolves.* ⁴ *Do not take a purse or bag or sandals; and do not greet anyone on the road.* ⁵ *"When you enter a house, first say, 'Peace to this house.'* ⁶ *If someone who promotes peace is there, your peace will rest on them; if not, it will return to you.* ⁷ *Stay there, eating and drinking whatever they give you, for the worker deserves his wages. Do not move around from house to house.* ⁸ *"When you enter a town and are welcomed, eat what is offered to you.* ⁹ *Heal the sick who are there and tell them, 'The kingdom of God has come near to you.'* ¹⁰ *But when you enter a town and are not welcomed, go into its streets and say,* ¹¹ *'Even the dust of your town we wipe from our feet as a warning to you. Yet be sure of this: The kingdom of God has come near.'* ¹² *I tell you, it will be more bearable on that day for Sodom than for that town. …* ¹⁷ *The seventy-two returned with joy and said, "Lord, even the demons submit to us in your name."* ¹⁸ *He replied, "I saw Satan fall like lightning from heaven.* ¹⁹ *I have given you authority to trample on snakes and scorpions and to overcome all the power of the enemy; nothing will harm you.* ²⁰ *However, do not rejoice that the spirits submit to you, but rejoice that your names are written in heaven."* ²¹ *At that time Jesus, full of joy through the Holy Spirit, said, "I praise you, Father, Lord of heaven and earth, because you have hidden these things from the wise and learned, and revealed them to little children. Yes, Father, for this is what you were pleased to do.* ²² *"All things have been committed to me by my Father. No one knows who the Son is except the Father, and no one knows who the Father is except the Son and those to whom the Son chooses to reveal him."* ²³ *Then he turned to his disciples and said privately, "Blessed are the eyes that see what you see.* ²⁴ *For I tell you that many prophets and kings wanted to see what you see but did not see it, and to hear what you hear but did not hear it."*

Text

Read through the above passage three times. Underline or highlight any words or phrases that jump out to you.

What phrases in this passage relate to Jesus' and our mission? *(List those verses or phrases below.)*

Immerse

Choose two or three phrases or verses to study further.
You might want to look up the definition for those words,
find out where those Greek words are used elsewhere
in the Scriptures, or study the theological and historical
context for those verses. Write a summary of your findings
below and then choose one verse to memorize this week.

PHRASE A:

INSIGHT:

PHRASE B:

INSIGHT:

PHRASE C:

INSIGHT:

MEMORY VERSE:

Ministry

Now that you have read and studied the text, what is the Spirit leading you to believe or do as a result? Why did the Spirit highlight those phrases or words? What is He trying to teach you about His people? How is He calling you to live as a result?

Encounter

With all of this in mind, take this to God in prayer. Use the space below to write out a prayer and also to write out anything you hear God saying as a result. Then close your time by writing out a song/poem of praise to God.

MY PRAYER:

LISTENING:

MY SONG OF PRAISE:

05

Power

"*Many people feel so pressured by the expectations of others that it causes them to be frustrated, miserable, and confused about what they should do. But there is a way to live a simple, joy-filled, peaceful life, and the key is learning how to be led by the Holy Spirit, not the traditions or expectations of man.*"
— *Joyce Meyers*

Much of our current culture and economy is built on the idea that one should work hard and make something of themselves; that each of us should seek to live a life of consequence through personal achievement. We are encouraged to develop personal drive so we can accomplish more, make more money, and work harder—harder than we did yesterday, and harder than those around us. Working hard can be an honorable act if it is done in the right direction and out of the right motivation. Sadly, our culture often encourages us to be motivated by pride, greed, and gluttony, and to find our personal drive and power within ourselves—believing that personal drive and power can be cultivated by us, for us, and from us.

Unfortunately, the drive to always be successful and live the "good life" by working harder than we did yesterday often leads to fatigue, exhaustion, and guilt. In working harder and pushing ourselves, we eventually reach our own personal limits—the limits of our body, our mind, and our emotions. When we hit our limits—or crash and burn—we feel frustration, exhaustion, and shame. This sense of failure leads us to quit, which furthers our sense of failure, leading to guilt which prompts us to once again try and work harder. A prime example of this "work harder" cycle is the poem displayed in the New York City Times Square station for over a quarter of a century, entitled "A Commuter's Lament." Each line of the poem is hung above commuters' heads every 10 or so feet apart. It reads:

> *Overslept,*
> *So tired.*
> *If late,*
> *Get fired.*
> *Why bother?*
> *Why the pain?*
> *Just go home.*
> *Do it again.*

As the poet Norman Colp wryly suggests, we are forever stuck in a "do it again" loop of exhaustion, frustration, and depression.

Even if we do experience some success by being self-motivated and hard-working, the success we achieve and the pleasures we enjoy as a result have diminishing returns. We need a little more money, a little more sex, and an even better vacation to experience the same pleasure we did last time. This law of diminishing returns was demonstrated by Wilhelm Wundt in the 19th century through his study of stimulus intensity, and how stimuli can move from pleasant, to comfortable, to unpleasant. In the 1970s, Daniel E. Berlyne published a study that showed how quickly the pleasure of something new wears off. In both studies, although initial stimulus and novelty led to pleasure, overall pleasure experienced by participants decreased over time. As C.S. Lewis summarizes in his book **The Screwtape Letters**, we have "an ever-increasing craving for an ever-diminishing pleasure."

Despite all our efforts and hard work, we seem unable to get ahold of the "carrot" our culture places in front of us, leading us to strive more and turn to new ways of coping and surviving. At first, we may try to self-medicate through pleasure, but soon this turns into addictions, escapes, and increasingly empty or dark sin patterns because we are never truly satisfied or sustained. This is what the apostle Paul called the desires of the flesh and the acts of the flesh (i.e., what we do in our own strength to try to satisfy our own broken desires):

> *So I say, walk by the Spirit, and you will not gratify the desires of the flesh. For the flesh desires what is contrary to the Spirit, and the Spirit what is contrary to the flesh…The acts of the flesh are obvious: sexual immorality, impurity and debauchery; idolatry and witchcraft; hatred, discord, jealousy, fits of rage, selfish ambition, dissensions, factions and envy; drunkenness, orgies, and the like. I warn you, as I did before, that those who live like this will not inherit the kingdom of God. (Gal. 5:16–7a, 19–21)*

All these acts of the flesh are simply an attempt to find strength and life outside of God. In this way, they are all forms of idolatry—humanity trying to find its satisfaction and life from someone or something other than God.

Even within the Church we can fall into a similar trap. Although we have received forgiveness and everlasting life in and through the work of Christ, we can buy into the lie that now we have to obey Jesus and provide for ourselves out of our own strength. We adopt the adage "God helps those who help themselves," and believe that we should do everything in our own strength until we face a huge obstacle, and then—and only then—we should pray and ask God to help.

This way of life is a form of striving. We tell ourselves that if we can suck it up, try harder, discipline ourselves further, and pursue the Scriptures with more vigor, then everything will be fine and we will become "good Christians" with "good lives." It's true that growth does come through effort, but often, the way we go about things and the power that we rely on are unsustainable. We end up trusting in our own efforts, and soon our souls begin to wither. The phrase that gets to the heart of the issue is "burn out." We try to maintain moral standards, only to give into temptation; we seek to be kind to people, only to give into anger and frustration; we seek to serve the poor, only to get caught up in our own needs and desires.

Whether we realize it or not, this way of life is a type of religious legalism. We try to force ourselves *externally* to follow the laws of God, as if we can somehow make ourselves righteous in God's eyes. But the Christian life is not designed to be run by willpower, drive, or even a vision of making an impact; it is meant to be powered by the love of Jesus that comes through intimate union with His Spirit in your innermost being. The Christian life is meant to be lived from the inside out— by the power of the Spirit and not the power of the self (or flesh). The Holy Spirit wants to work *in us* to will and act according to His purposes, yet we often refuse to listen to or rely upon the Spirit. This is exactly the sin pattern Paul calls out in the Galatian church: "Are you so foolish? After beginning by means of the Spirit, are you now trying to finish by means of the flesh?" (Gal. 3:3)

It is folly and arrogance that lead us to believe that we can somehow obey God in our own strength. This self-effort creates an unhealthy Church built on the foundations of a broken under-standing of the Gospel. Not only is this type of church unhealthy, but religious legalism also leads to exhaustion, because it is impossible to obey God apart from the Spirit. Jesus says this quite clearly in John 15:5–6: "Apart from Me you can do nothing. If you do not remain in Me, you are like a branch that is thrown away and withers; such branches are picked up, thrown into the fire and burned."

Abiding in Jesus

When Jesus walked the earth, He looked around His Jewish community and saw the same idolatry and exhaustion we experience today. In response to the people's exhaustion, Jesus said, "Come to Me, all you who are weary and burdened, and I will give you rest. Take My yoke upon you and learn from me, for I am gentle and humble in heart, and you will find rest for your souls. For My yoke is easy and My burden is light" (Matt. 11:28–30). In saying this, Jesus was offering the people a new way to live life and obey God. Instead of attempting to obey God and fulfill the commandments in their own strength, they could go to Jesus and attach themselves to Him; they could give Him their burdens and in return yoke themselves (like a pair of oxen) to Jesus, who would give them the strength to live a holy life.

Similarly, Jesus told His disciples to "Remain in Me, as I also remain in you. No branch can bear fruit by itself; it must remain in the vine...As the Father has loved Me, so have I loved you. Now remain in My love" (John 15:4–9). When Jesus says that He is the vine, He is saying that He is the source of our life. It is His power, grace, love, mercy, and presence that flow through us and produce the fruit that He desires. Like a flower that withers when it is cut from its roots, we cannot produce lasting fruit apart from Him. In his book Holy in Christ, Andrew Murray writes: "However strong the branch becomes, however far away it reaches round the home, out of sight of the vine, all its beauty and all its fruitfulness ever depend upon that one point of contact where it grows out of the vine. So be it with us too."

In inviting His disciples to yoke themselves to Him and to remain in His love as a branch remains attached to a vine, Jesus was offering His followers the chance to abide in Him—to live and rest in His presence. For the disciples, abiding with Jesus first involved spending time with Him and traveling with Him throughout the country. But after His ascension, abiding with Jesus meant studying the Scriptures, praying, listening to Jesus's voice through the indwelling presence of the Spirit, and spending time with others in communal worship, fellowship, and evangelism. The same is true for us today. To abide in Jesus is to invite Him into every aspect of our life, and to find our purpose, identity, and nourishment in His presence. The beautiful, flourishing, restful yet productive life we each long for can only be found by first abiding in Jesus. All other wells of life that we attempt to dig for ourselves are "broken cisterns" that cannot hold life or live up to the demands of life (Jer. 2:13). This is why John Ortberg so rightly concludes: "Any time you see life flourishing, it is because it is receiving nourishment from outside of itself." So, too, we are invited to receive nourishment and life outside of ourselves.

So how do we remain in Jesus and live out of His power?
How can we live lives of joy and fruitfulness, instead of
exhaustion and guilt?

The life and power of Christ are made accessible through
the indwelling person of the Holy Spirit. As 1 John 4:13
states, "This is how we know that we live in [Jesus] and
He in us: He has given us of His Spirit." The Holy Spirit
is the One who enables us to abide and live in His love;
He is the One who empowers us to live abundant lives
of fruitfulness, service, and mission. It is the Spirit Who
invites us into the very presence of God to enjoy forever
communion with Him. With this in mind, let's turn now to
the person of the Holy Spirit.

The Person of the Holy Spirit

One of the reasons we can fall into the trap of living the
Christian life in our own strength is because we do not truly
know or understand the Holy Spirit. As theologian Thomas
C. Oden states, "The modern tendency is to depersonalize
the Spirit, to treat God the Spirit as reducible to a general
idea of spirituality." If we think the Holy Spirit is an imper-
sonal force, then we will be unwilling to rely upon the Spirit
to help us overcome the challenges of life. But as Jesus so
clearly teaches in John chapters 14 to 16, the Holy Spirit is
a person with thoughts, emotions, plans, and the power to
fulfill those plans. Jesus calls the Holy Spirit the Counselor,
Helper, and Advocate, and then tells His disciples that it's
better to have the Spirit with them than to have Jesus with
them! D. L. Moody summarizes the Scriptures' teachings
regarding the person and work of the Spirit: "The work of the
Spirit is to impart life, to implant hope, to give liberty, to testify of Christ, to guide us into all truth, to teach us all things,
to comfort the believer, and to convict the world of sin."

After we recognize the personhood of the Holy Spirit, we then need to recognize the miracle that occurred at Pentecost—the Spirit came to live with and in us. Just as Jesus entered our world, taking on flesh and living among us, so also the Holy Spirit, on the day of Pentecost, became incarnate. The Spirit descended from heaven and took up residence in each of the disciples' bodies, appearing visually like a flame of fire and auditorily like a rushing wind (reminiscent of when God descended on Mount Sinai). The flesh the Spirit put on is the flesh of every one of Jesus's disciples. This is why Paul writes: "Do you not know that your bodies are temples of the Holy Spirit, Who is in you, Whom you have received from God? You are not your own; you were bought at a price. Therefore honor God with your bodies" (1 Cor. 6:19–20). In 2 Corinthians 6:16, Paul reiterates this point when he says, "For we are the temple of the living God. As God has said: 'I will live with them and walk among them, and I will be their God, and they will be My people.'" The Greek word Paul uses for "temple" carries the idea that our bodies and souls are not simply the general temple grounds, but the very Holy of Holies, where God's presence spoke from above the mercy seat (Num. 7:89).

In the teachings of Jesus and Paul, and in the stories of the early church recorded in Acts, we learn that the Holy Spirit is meant to take up residence in every believer, not just a select few. In the past, the Spirit would come upon prophets, judges, and kings for a short time and with a specific mission; after Pentecost, the Spirit is now given to all believers to empower every man, woman, and child for supernatural ministry in God's kingdom. This is what Peter emphasizes in the beginning of his famous Pentecost sermon: "'I will pour out My Spirit on all people. Your sons and daughters will prophesy, your young men will see visions, your old men will dream dreams. Even on My servants, both men and women, I will pour out My Spirit in those days'...The promise is for you and your children and for all who are far off—for all whom the Lord our God will call" (Acts 2:17–18, 39). The Spirit is not given to a few spiritual elites who have mastered their faith and secured a place amongst the Christian masters; the Spirit is given freely as a promise to everyone who is in the kingdom of God—that's what makes life in the new covenant so extraordinary. Everyone is filled with the Spirit and moving in power—prophesying, seeing visions, proclaiming the gospel with boldness, sharing their possessions with gladness, and seeing miracles performed in their midst (Acts 2:42–47; 4:31–35). The first Christians were marked by the Spirit, by the power of God among them. As Francis Chan notes: "When you read the New Testament, you see the Holy Spirit was supposed to change everything so that this gathering of people who call themselves Christians had this supernatural element about them."

Spirit-led Abundant Life

Just as Jesus told His disciples to abide in Him like a branch to a vine in order to receive life, it is in fact the person of the Holy Spirit living inside us that is the life-giving power flowing through us to produce abundant life. In John 7:38–39a Jesus declares, "Whoever believes in Me, as Scripture has said, rivers of living water will flow from within them." In saying this, Jesus was speaking about the Holy Spirit's refreshing work in our life. Likewise, in John 4:13–14, Jesus says, "Everyone who drinks this water will be thirsty again, but whoever drinks the water I give them will never thirst. Indeed, the water I give them will become in them a spring of water welling up to eternal life." Through the Spirit we are empowered to live the abundant life Jesus promised His disciples. The Spirit will be like a well of living water that is flowing through us, bringing life and vitality to every part of ourselves and our life. This refreshing water will also flow out of us, as the Spirit works to bring life to those we interact with.

We experience abundance (i.e., the fruits of the Spirit) both for ourselves and for those around us. As we discover the love of God, this love flows out of us to other people. As we experience a Spirit-given peace and joy that surpasses our circumstances, this peace and joy then begins to permeate our lives and interactions. As we experience God's patience with us, then the Spirit empowers us to be patient with others. The abundant, fruitful life is a gift to us and begins to be good news to those around us. This new life (of love, joy, peace, patience, kindness, goodness, faithfulness, gentleness, and self-control) is not a matter of self-driven behavior management. No, it comes from spending time in God's presence and listening to the voice of the Spirit.

Not only is the Spirit described as refreshing life-giving water, but He is the very breath in us giving new life to our spirits. Just as God breathed into Adam giving Him life, so the Spirit breathes into us giving us new life. The Holy Spirit gives life to our dead spirits and then He continues to lead us into the abundant life Jesus promised us. Like David wrote, "He leads me beside quiet waters, He refreshes my soul" (Ps. 23:2b–3a).

But if we cannot see the Spirit, how can we follow the Spirit? In John 3:7–8, Jesus compares the movement of the Spirit to the wind: "You should not be surprised at My saying, 'You must be born again.' The wind blows wherever it pleases. You hear its sound, but you cannot tell where it comes from or where it is going. So it is with everyone born of the Spirit." Jesus plays upon the various meanings of the Greek word pneuma. Like its Hebrew counterpart (ruach), pneuma can mean wind, breath, spirit, or Spirit, as in the Spirit of God. In the Old Testament, the Spirit of God was often described as rushing upon or coming upon someone (like a mighty wind), or as filling a person (like a lung-full of air, or a sail in the wind). But this was only ever for a short time, and often happened to unexpected and unsuspecting people. In the New Testament, Jesus promises that the Holy Spirit will come upon all those who are born again and will remain in them, but that the Spirit won't lose His original "windy, breathy" quality. The Spirit will still move through people in unexpected, uncontrollable ways that are beyond human prediction or understanding. Being led by the Spirit is like a ship being carried along by the wind (2 Pet. 1:21). We must learn to wait upon the Spirit's movement, to seek to be filled with Him, and to move wherever He is moving. Like a good sailor, we want to be ever ready to respond to the winds of the Spirit.

The Bible describes being led by the Spirit as walking by or keeping in step with the Spirit (Gal. 5:16). This is a moment-by-moment leading as you follow Him. Like a dancer keeping in step with and being led by her partner, following the Spirit can be a life of faith and freedom. Joyce Meyer wisely wrote: "Many people feel so pressured by the expectations of others that it causes them to be frustrated, miserable and confused about what they should do. But there is a way to live a simple, joy-filled, peaceful life, and the key is learning how to be led by the Holy Spirit, not the traditions or expectations of man."

Each day we have the choice to be led by the Spirit or to run after other things. Each day we have the choice to be filled with the breath of the Spirit, allowing His life-giving love and power to permeate every part of us so that we are "filled to the measure of all the fullness of God" (Eph. 3:19), or to run after other sources of life and power, becoming–once again–broken, empty, dry cisterns (Jer. 2:13). Paul urges us to choose fullness:

> Be very careful, then, how you live—not as unwise but as wise, making the most of every opportunity, because the days are evil. Therefore do not be foolish, but understand what the Lord's will is. Do not get drunk on wine, which leads to debauchery. Instead, be filled with the Spirit, speaking to one another with psalms, hymns, and songs from the Spirit. Sing and make music from your heart to the Lord, always giving thanks to God the Father for everything, in the name of our Lord Jesus Christ. (Eph. 5:15–20)

The Christian life is not meant to be lived dryly or wearily, but to be a life of overflowing water and rushing wind, filled with the presence of God.

The Holy Spirit is willing and ready to empower us and fill us every day as we invite Him into our mind, heart, and circumstances. No longer do we have to live lives of exhaustion, defeat, or legalism. Instead, each day we can invite the Spirit to fill us and empower us to do His will. We can turn to God in prayer at any time of day or as many times as we need to throughout the day, inviting the Spirit to once again empower us as we rest in Him. So, whenever you sense that you have returned to living out of your own strength, confess this to God and then invite the Holy Spirit to once again lead, guide, and empower you. As Saint Augustine declared, "O Holy Spirit, descend plentifully into my heart. Enlighten the dark corners of this neglected dwelling and scatter there Thy cheerful beams."

To trust in God—to live and walk by the Spirit—is to live counter-culturally; it is to live as a completely new type of human. And when, as a Spirit-filled Christian, the Spirit's power and love flows through you, your life becomes supernormal ("exceeding or beyond the normal; exceptional") and supernatural ("exceeding or beyond the natural; of divine origin"), pointing to a better, eternal life offered through Jesus *(The Oxford Dictionary)*.

In His Presence

The Spirit's deepest desire is to glorify God and draw us into His presence. Although being empowered to be Jesus' people in a broken world is certainly a large part of how the Spirit moves in power in our life (and we will look at that more below), the eternal desire of the Spirit is to draw us into the presence of God so we can forever worship and commune with Him. To this end, the Spirit is the deposit and guarantee of our future. He is God dwelling in us now, the presence of God in us, as a sign that one day we will forever live in the Presence of God, finally seeing Him face to face.

It is the Spirit who enables us to pray, to worship, to hear God's voice, and to experience God's deep love and delight in us. We pray because the Spirit prompts us to pray and then prays through us, translating our wordless groans and desires into the language of heaven (Rom. 8:26). We worship because the Spirit worships through us, always declaring the glory of the Father and Son. As Jesus explains in John 4:23–24: "Yet a time is coming and has now come when the true worshipers will worship the Father in the Spirit and in truth, for they are the kind of worshipers the Father seeks. God is spirit, and his worshipers must worship in the Spirit and in truth."

The deep longing of the Spirit is for us to draw near to God, to live in intimate communion with Him. The intimacy your heart longs for is found by leaning into the Spirit through prayer and worship, through rest and service, whether you're in the midst of mourning or celebration. More than acts of service, the Lord wants you in His presence now—to taste here on earth what it is like in the heavens; to experience the abundant intimate life now that you will have with Him for all of eternity.

If the Spirit desires for all of us to experience intimate communion, then why do so many Christians experience "dry" spiritual lives? Why do so few Christians pray and worship? A.W. Tozer explains:

> *Why do some persons 'find' God in a way that others do not? Why does God manifest His Presence to some and let multitudes of others struggle along in the half-light of imperfect Christian experience? Of course the will of God is the same for all. He has no favorites within His household. All He has ever done for any of His children He will do for all of His children. The difference lies not with God but with us.* (*The Pursuit of God*)

If the difference lies with us, then how do we practice being in God's presence? How can we lean into the Spirit's leading, moving in step with and not against Him?

Developing a Rule of Life

Often one of the keys to spiritual growth is developing what past generations of Christians called a "rule of life." Using this mindset, practicing God's presence involves habits, daily and weekly rhythms, and breakthrough events.

Brother Lawrence, who lived during the 1600s, encouraged his generation to "practice the presence of God" by continually conversing with God in the depth of the center of their soul. Brother Lawrence knew that intimacy with God came through the habitual return to God's presence, the ongoing reliance upon the Holy Spirit. In the same way, we can learn to practice being in the presence of the God who is ever-present with us throughout our days.

Begin by cultivating short little "pockets of presence" throughout your day when you turn off all technology and instead meditate upon the Scriptures and listen to God. Maybe 10 minutes on your commute to work, 10 minutes at lunch, 10 minutes on your break, and 10 minutes before you go to bed. As Brother Lawrence instructs in *The Practice of the Presence of God*, "Lift up your heart to Him during your meals and in company; the least little remembrance will always be the most pleasing to Him. One need not cry out very loudly; He is nearer to us than we think."

Practicing the presence of God also involves daily and weekly rhythms. Christians in past generations installed the "daily office" to help them set aside three times a day to stop their normal activities and turn to God in prayer. Likewise, the Israelite priests had set times each day when they would offer sacrifices in the Temple and worship God. In modern-day America we can still institute these practices through daily hours of prayer, set times of Scripture study, and regular times for reflection. Whether for 15 minutes or an hour, we can create rhythms of worship.

Along with daily rhythms, the Scriptures show us the importance of weekly rhythms. In Exodus 16 and Leviticus 23, the Lord commands the Israelites to set aside one whole day each week to rest and worship Him. The weekly Sabbath was meant to be an ongoing reminder that there was a future Sabbath-rest promised for God's people, when they would no longer sweat and struggle, but would forever worship in God's presence. God knew that they needed to be reminded each week that His ultimate goal for their lives was being in His presence.

As modern-day Christians it is still vital to our spiritual health to practice the Sabbath. By setting aside a whole day to rest and worship, we are actively seeking to abide in the Spirit's presence. The goal of the Sabbath, and of attending a Sunday church service, is not to gather together with people for play and community, but to enter into God's presence. As Philip Yancey writes: "Church exists primarily not to provide entertainment or to encourage vulnerability or to build self-esteem or to facilitate friendships but to worship God; if it fails in that, it fails. I have learned that the ministers, the music, the sacraments, and the other 'trappings' of worship are mere promptings to support the ultimate goal of getting worshipers in touch with God."

Along with habits and daily and weekly rhythms, we need breakthrough events ("mountain-top moments") when we encounter the presence and power of God in a deeply meaningful, extended way. Some of these breakthrough moments will come upon us unexpectedly when the Spirit moves in power. (Think of the three disciples on the mountain with Jesus, when the Spirit suddenly exposes Jesus' true glory, or when the apostle John is given a vision of the resurrected Lord in heaven). Other times in life, we can plan and structure these breakthrough events. In Leviticus 23, God declares a series of longer holidays for the Jewish people to celebrate each year, when they are to travel to Jerusalem for a week-long festival at the Temple. Although these were anticipated moments, they were still deeply meaningful times of entering God's presence with worship, prayer, and sacrifices.

How might the Spirit be prompting you to set aside times each year for spiritual retreats when you can spend extended time in His presence? It is in these hours of prayer and worship that we truly lean into the profound love of the Father, Son, and Spirit. No longer getting quick moments of refreshing, we can truly be overwhelmed and astonished as the Holy Spirit pours out on us hour after hour. It is in these places that the Spirit begins to give us a deep hunger for His presence, as we learn to be unsatisfied by the fleeting passions of earth or small glimpses of His presence. Like David, we will begin to say, "As the deer pants for streams of water, so my soul pants for You, my God. My soul thirsts for God, for the living God. When can I go and meet with God?" (Ps. 42:1–2) and, "One thing I ask from the Lord, this only do I seek: that I may dwell in the house of the Lord all the days of my life, to gaze on the beauty of the Lord and to seek Him in His temple." (Ps. 27:4). David became a man who was no longer satisfied by Sabbaths or seasonal week-long holidays at the Temple; he wanted to always be in the Presence of God, always filled with the Holy Spirit, forever basking in the beauty of the Lord. The Spirit can cultivate in us this same longing after God's own heart. A.W. Tozer concludes, "To have found God and still to pursue Him is the soul's paradox of love, scorned indeed by the too easily satisfied religionist, but justified in happy experience by the children of the burning fire."

Empowered Living

Not only are we invited to enter in the presence of the Lord and be led by His Spirit, but we are invited to act out of His strength—to be empowered for holy living. The Scriptures say that the same power that raised Jesus from the dead—namely the Holy Spirit—is at work in each of our lives as well (Romans 8:11). When the Spirit not only dwells in our hearts, but also—in response to our faith and abiding—fills us, then we are empowered to live in the way of Jesus and to do even greater works than He did! Jesus says that we will do even greater works, because He too loved and acted out of the Holy Spirit's power. Jesus modeled for us Spirit-reliant, Spirit-empowered living. Jesus did not begin His ministry until He received the Holy Spirit during His baptism (Matt. 3:16). It was the Spirit who led Him into the wilderness to be tested and who moved through Jesus in power to heal the sick (Luke 4:1; 8:46). Jesus showed how we are meant to live and what the "new normal" would be for humanity—Spirit-empowered living!

So what does the Spirit empower us to do? He empowers us to bear fruit, serve the Body, and bring His kingdom.

Empowered to Bear Fruit

Jesus says to His disciples in John 15:16, "You did not choose Me, but I chose you and appointed you so that you might go and bear fruit—fruit that will last—and so that whatever you ask in My name the Father will give you." The Spirit empowers us to bear the fruit of righteousness, the fruit of the Spirit, and the fruit of endurance.

The Spirit empowers us to bear the fruit of righteousness (Eph. 5:9)—or obedience to God—by teaching us, guiding us, and giving us the desire to live a life pleasing to Him. In John 14:26 Jesus states, "But the Advocate, the Holy Spirit, Whom the Father will send in My name, will teach you all things and will remind you of everything I have said to you." The Spirit teaches and explains the Scriptures, so we can understand God's instructions. He illuminates God's words and uses them to train and correct us. The Spirit reminds us of God's Word throughout the day, prompting our minds with the Scriptures we have studied. By teaching us God's commands and reminding us to obey them, the Spirit leads us in the way of Jesus and begins to transform our habits, desires, and thoughts by renewing our mind (Rom. 12:2).

Likewise, the Spirit also convicts and corrects us when we are disobeying and producing the fruit of the flesh (Rom. 7:5). Jesus says in John 16, "But very truly I tell you, it is for your good that I am going away. Unless I go away, the Advocate will not come to you; but if I go, I will send Him to you. When He comes, He will prove the world to be in the wrong about sin and righteousness and judgment... But when He, the Spirit of truth, comes, He will guide you into all the truth." Jesus uses the Greek word elegchó to describe this work of the Spirit, a verb meaning "to expose, to convict, or reprove." Elsewhere in the Scriptures, this same work of the Spirit is described as the exposure created by light shining in the darkness (John 3:20; Eph. 5:11–13), and as a sword cutting and piercing the heart (Acts 2:37; 5:33; 7:54).

You and I do not need to obey God out of our own strength, mustering up the desire and willpower to obey Him each and every moment, telling ourselves to "try harder" and "be better." Instead, we can choose to live by faith, trusting in the Holy Spirit to empower us, providing us with "everything we need for a godly life" (2 Pet. 1:3). It is the Spirit who works in us "to will and to act in order to fulfill His good purpose" (Phil. 2:13).

As we learn from the Spirit how to obey God, He then produces in us the fruits of the Spirit. The fruit of the Spirit—not the fruit of self-effort but the fruit of dependency upon the Spirit's work in and through us—is "love, joy, peace, forbearance, kindness, goodness, faithfulness, gentleness and self-control. Against such things there is no law" (Gal. 5:22–23). In calling these attributes "fruits of the Spirit," Paul makes it clear that we cannot manifest these qualities through our own self-effort. Despite what the world may tell us, our natural selves cannot produce love or patience or kindness. In our own strength these will always be twisted or tainted by selfishness and sin. Only the God of love can produce true love.

Finally, as Jesus states in John 15:16, it is the Spirit Who empowers and enables us to produce fruit that lasts. One of the promises in the book of Revelation is that in the New Jerusalem there will be trees planted along the river flowing out from the Throne of God which will bear fruit and leaves (for the healing of the nations) in every season (Rev. 22:2). This same image is used in Psalm 1:3 of a person who delights in the Lord: "That person is like a tree planted by streams of water, which yields its fruit in season and whose leaf does not wither—whatever they do prospers." You and I are meant to be people who delight in the Lord and plant ourselves along the living waters of the Holy Spirit. As Spirit-filled water gets into our lives, we not only bear fruit, but we also bear it in every season of life— winter and summer, in times of joy and times of suffering.

It is the Holy Spirit that empowers us to endure hardships and also remain steady and faithful over the course of our life. Colossians 1:9b–11 reads, "We continually ask God to fill you with the knowledge of His will through all the wisdom and understanding that the Spirit gives... bearing fruit in every good work, growing in the knowledge of God, being strengthened with all power according to His glorious might so that you may have great endurance and patience." The Holy Spirit is our forever help Who will teach, lead, give, fill, and empower us for our entire lives, if we will simply let Him.

May the words of Isaiah 40:28–31 be true for us: "Do you not know? Have you not heard? The Lord is the everlasting God, the Creator of the ends of the earth. He will not grow tired or weary, and His understanding no one can fathom. He gives strength to the weary and increases the power of the weak. Even youths grow tired and weary, and young men stumble and fall; but those who hope in the Lord will renew their strength. They will soar on wings like eagles; they will run and not grow weary, they will walk and not be faint." The Spirit is the One Who strengthens our weary arms, increases our power when we feel weak, fills us with His breath to continue the life-long journey of obedience, and produces His fruit in our life in every season.

Empowered to Serve the Body

Along with bearing fruit in our own life, the Spirit also empowers us to serve the Body of Christ, the community of local believers. Paul, in his various epistles, often employs the image of a "body" to explain the relationship between the Church and Jesus, and the relationships between various believers within the Church. Jesus is the head of the church, like a head to a body; every person in the church is like a different part of that body, each having their own unique role to play and yet dependent upon all the others. Romans 12:4–5 states: "For just as each of us has one body with many members, and these members do not all have the same function, so in Christ we, though many, form one body, and each member belongs to all the others."

In Romans 12, 1 Corinthians 12, Ephesians 4, and 1 Peter 4, Paul explains that it is the Holy Spirit who forms us into the Body of Christ. To that end, the Spirit empowers the

Body in two ways: by distributing spiritual gifts to every believer and by supernaturally uniting the various members of the church (and the various churches across the world) into one unified Body.

In regard to spiritual gifts, Paul explains:

> *Now about the gifts of the Spirit, brothers and sisters, I do not want you to be uninformed...There are different kinds of gifts, but the same Spirit distributes them. There are different kinds of service, but the same Lord. There are different kinds of working, but in all of them and in everyone it is the same God at work. Now to each one the manifestation of the Spirit is given for the common good. To one there is given through the Spirit a message of wisdom, to another a message of knowledge by means of the same Spirit, to another faith by the same Spirit, to another gifts of healing by that one Spirit, to another miraculous powers, to another prophecy, to another distinguishing between spirits, to another speaking in different kinds of tongues, and to still another the interpretation of tongues. All these are the work of one and the same Spirit, and He distributes them to each one, just as He determines. Just as a body, though one, has many parts, but all its many parts form one body, so it is with Christ. (1 Cor. 12:1; 4–12)*

From this text, we learn that spiritual gifts are Holy Spirit-given abilities to serve the Christian community. They are given not expressly for the sake of the individual (though a person may get some benefit from their own gift), but rather to benefit the church and to work together for the advancement of God's kingdom. Everyone is given a gift by the Holy Spirit and so everyone has a part to play in Jesus's Body. In other words, the Body of Christ would not be the same without you!

Other names for spiritual gifts are "manifestations of the Spirit" or "grace gifts." This wording emphasizes the fact that spiritual gifts are not derived from our natural abilities, personalities, or our own righteousness, but are purely a result of the Spirit's power at work in and through us. In this sense a spiritual gift is a supernatural, extraordinary ability that comes from the Spirit's power and which advances His purposes in the world. Someone may be a naturally friendly person, but a person relying upon the Spirit's gift of hospitality has a way of making others feel like Jesus Himself is welcoming them in. A person might work as a teacher professionally and have worldly training in communication, but when someone filled with the Spirit has the gift of teaching, their words seem to cut to the heart as the Spirit Himself moves through the spoken word to the heart and mind of the listener. Therefore, a person cannot truly operate in their spiritual gift without, in the moment, relying upon the Holy Spirit's power.

This reality is even more obvious in the so-called "supernatural gifts" (which is really a misnomer, since all spiritual gifts are supernatural) of healing, miracles, tongues, prophecy, and discernment. A person cannot lay hands on someone and see the healing power of Jesus break out without moving in the power of the Holy Spirit. It was the Spirit who moved through Jesus to perform miracles, and it is the same with His disciples. This is why, in Matthew 9, a woman grabs the hem of Jesus's robe and healing power flows through Jesus and into her, without Jesus even knowing He was grabbed; it was the Spirit doing this through Him. The same happens in Acts 19 when people are healed by touching handkerchiefs and aprons that Paul has touched; it's the Spirit Who performs the miracle, not Paul directly.

The Lord longs to bring healing, freedom, prophecy, love, and teaching (and all the gifts) into our world, but this will only come as His people rely upon the power of the Holy Spirit to perform signs and wonders through themselves. Jesus wants to bring His kingdom into the midst of His people, and the Holy Spirit wants to do this by pouring Himself out in power in and through His people. The day of Pentecost and the early days of the church were meant to be an ongoing reality for the people of God—the sick being healed, the hungry fed, the gospel being proclaimed with boldness, and the church growing through the power of the Spirit.

Because spiritual gifts are the power of the Spirit flowing through you to bring life to others, operating in the power of the Spirit is truly life-giving work. It is life-giving to those who benefit from your spiritual gift and it is often life-giving to you, as the Spirit moves through you. This is where the teaching of Jesus in John 7:38–39 is so true: "'Whoever believes in Me, as Scripture has said, rivers of living water will flow from within them.' By this He meant the Spirit, Whom those who believed in Him were later to receive." This is why Paul urges his readers to discover their gifts, to grow in their gifts, and to eagerly desire the gifts. In order to fully experience our new life in Jesus, we must rely upon the Spirit to bring His resurrection life into our life and into the lives of those around us.

As many believers in a local church begin to lean into the power of the Spirit, He works to use all of the gifts to build up the Body into a mature, unified whole. The Holy Spirit distributes gifts so that "the body of Christ may be built up until we all reach unity in the faith and in the knowledge of the Son of God and become mature, attaining to the whole measure of the fullness of Christ" (Eph. 4:12b–13). The Spirit's goal is a unified, mature, Christ-like Church. The church is not meant to be a random group of individuals all doing their own thing because it's "just me and Jesus."

No, we have been called to be a people, a holy nation, a body that is working together to bring God's kingdom on earth as it is in heaven. But we cannot be a unified body without the help and power of the Spirit.

When we rely upon our own strength and understanding, there are internal divisions, cliques, unforgiveness, and rifts that appear in the church. Without the power of the Spirit, we cannot overcome our differences (of opinion and upbringing) to form one, unified people. Only the Spirit, one Person in a triune God who knows perfect unity within the Godhead, can bring true unity from diversity.

The early church faced similar obstacles as we do today. They were living in a society that was segregated by race, class, gender, wealth, and physical abilities. However, they saw people of all types gathering together around the table to break bread together. People whom Roman and Jewish societies would never have seen together became brothers and sisters in Christ as the Spirit united them. This is why Paul could write, "For we were all baptized by one Spirit so as to form one body— whether Jews or Gentiles, slave or free—and we were all given the one Spirit to drink" (1 Cor. 12:13a).

We can see this same move of the Spirit today if we will humbly submit ourselves to the Spirit. It is the Spirit who can teach us how to love and to forgive, how to consider others better than ourselves and how to value every part of the Body. As we rely upon the outpouring of the Spirit's love and power "speaking the truth in love, we will grow to become in every respect the mature body of Him who is the head, that is, Christ. From Him the whole body, joined and held together by every supporting ligament, grows and builds itself up in love, as each part does its work" (Eph. 4:15–16).

A diverse group of people loving and serving together as one would be a true miracle, and perhaps our most compelling witness to society. Only the power of the Holy Spirit can accomplish such a task, which is why Jesus says that the world will know we are His disciples by our love for one another (John 13:35). A love like this is only made possible by a supernatural God.

Empowered to Bring the Kingdom

As the Spirit builds us into Christ's body, He then empowers us to be Jesus's hands and feet in our world, bringing His kingdom on earth as it is in heaven. In Acts 1, when Jesus commissions His disciples to go into all the world proclaiming and bringing God's kingdom (just as He had done), He tells them to wait until they are given the Holy Spirit: "But you will receive power when the Holy Spirit comes on you; and you shall be My witnesses" (Acts 1:8). Jesus knew that they could not proclaim the good news, make disciples, perform signs and wonders, or pray for more workers without the Holy Spirit empowering them for this ministry.

The same is still true for us today; we are not meant to make disciples or bring God's kingdom in our own strength. We are not meant to muster up enough courage to share our faith and then try to convince others to believe in Jesus. We are not meant to care for the sick and needy with our own strategies and social justice fervor. No, we are meant to rely upon the Spirit to prompt us, to anoint our preaching, and to empower our kingdom efforts.

As we see clearly in the book of Acts, it is the Spirit who empowers and blesses the work of evangelism. The Holy Spirit gives Jesus's disciples the courage (even when they are nervous or scared) to share their faith with boldness: "After they prayed, the place where they were meeting was shaken. And they were all filled with the Holy Spirit and spoke the word of God boldly" (Acts 4:31). This is what Jesus promised in Acts 1:8 and we see this in the life of Peter—a man who formerly denied Jesus during His crucifixion, returned to fishing after Jesus's resurrection, but then suddenly was brazenly courageous, proclaiming the gospel to hundreds after receiving the Holy Spirit on the day of Pentecost (Acts 2). Peter is also an example of how the Holy Spirit gives us the very words to share with others. The Spirit is the One who gives Peter the words to preach on Pentecost, who gives words to the disciples when they are brought before courts and rulers just as Jesus foretold, and who gives Paul the words to explain the gospel to the Gentiles (Luke 21:15; Acts 4:8; Acts 13:9). We are not meant to rely upon our own eloquent words or persuasive logic to convince others of the truth of the gospel. As Paul states: "My message and my preaching were not with wise and persuasive words, but with a demonstration of the Spirit's power, so that your faith might not rest on human wisdom, but on God's power" (1 Cor. 2:4–5). It is the Spirit Who prepares a person's heart to receive the good news of Jesus, and then Who testifies to the heart of the listener the truth of the gospel; we have very little to do with it (John 15:27; Acts 9:11; 16:9). Our job in evangelism is to pray for the Spirit's power and then to step out in faith, going to whoever and wherever He sends us.

As Paul mentions in 1 Corinthians 2, the Holy Spirit not only empowers the disciple and his or her words, but the Spirit confirms the message of the gospel with demonstrations of His power in signs and wonders. This is why Jesus commands His disciples to go into the towns and "heal the sick who are there and tell them, 'The kingdom of God has come near to you'" (Luke 10:9). Jesus knew that the Spirit wanted to confirm "His word by the signs that accompanied it" (Mark 16:20). Even after Jesus's resurrection, performing miracles was a normal part of the average disciple's evangelistic method. Stephen was not an apostle and yet he was "a man full of God's grace and power, [who] performed great wonders and signs among the people" (Acts 6:8).

Does this sound like the type of evangelism and discipleship you have been a part of?

If you are feeling overwhelmed or insecure, just remember that miracles and healings are the Spirit's power on display—not human effort. This is why, when the Spirit enables miracles and healings, it acts as confirmation that the message we are sharing is supernatural. Miracles alone are not the Spirit's desire (because even the devil can perform some wonders and imitate miracles); rather His desire is that every miracle is the accompaniment to the gospel—that people would hear the message of eternal life, and then see some example of life and healing in the temporary world.

Having said this, we need to ask the Spirit to move in power through us because there are many times where a miracle is a much "faster" solution to a very real problem or is the only solution to a human need. There are times when people need food and healing in order to know and believe in God's profound love for them. It is, of course, beautiful to serve the poor and fight injustice, but our human efforts alone will never solve these problems. We need the Spirit to accelerate the work of God's kingdom coming on earth. Even more so, there are times when only a demonstration of the Spirit's power will heal and free a desperate person—allowing them to even know Jesus themselves. For example, there are many in New York City who are suffering debilitating, incurable diseases, who are overcome by mental illnesses that make rational thought nearly impossible, or who are oppressed and possessed by demons. When Jesus was on earth he freed the oppressed, healed the invalids, and raised the dead. If we do not learn to move in the power of the Spirit, then people will never be freed or healed, or know the profound love of Jesus both here on earth and in eternity.

Just like the first disciples, this will be a learning process for us, of stepping out in faith and praying bold prayers. We might not always know who to pray for, how to pray, and how to move in the Spirit's power. Like the disciples, sometimes we won't pray effective prayers for healing and deliverance (Matt. 9:28), but this should not prevent us from continuing to pray and trusting Jesus. Jesus and the Spirit are inviting us to join Them; They have chosen us to be Jesus's hands and feet in the world. This is Jesus's plan for bringing His kingdom; who are we to not trust and obey?

This leads us into the final way that the Spirit empowers us for mission—He fuels our prayers with a hunger for God's kingdom to break out in our world. Only the Spirit can give us a holy imagination that dreams and yearns for the promises of Isaiah 61 to be fulfilled, not only in Jesus, but also through His Body, the church: "The Spirit of the Sovereign Lord is on me, because the Lord has anointed me to proclaim good news to the poor. He has sent me to bind up the brokenhearted, to proclaim freedom for the captives and release from darkness for the prisoners, to proclaim the year of the Lord's favor" (Isaiah 61:1–2a).

As we experience the power of the Spirit and His profound love for the lost, He moves in us to pray according to His will and not our own. These are prayers of love and compassion, prayers for more workers in "the harvest," prayers for His will to be done and for His kingdom to come (Luke 10:2; Matt 6:10). As we learn to long for others with the same longing as the Spirit, and to do kingdom work through the power of the Spirit, Jesus's words will be true in our life: "Very truly I tell you, whoever believes in Me will do the works I have been doing, and they will do even greater things than these, because I am going to the Father. And I will do whatever you ask in My name, so that the Father may be glorified in the Son. You may ask Me for anything in my name, and I will do it" (John 14:12–14). These are the prayers of faith, the prayers that are powerful and effective enough to heal the sick and save the sinner from death:

> *Is anyone among you in trouble? Let them pray. Is anyone happy? Let them sing songs of praise. Is anyone among you sick? Let them call the elders of the church to pray over them and anoint them with oil in the name of the Lord. And the prayer offered in faith will make the sick person well; the Lord will raise them up. If they have sinned, they will be forgiven. Therefore confess your sins to each other and pray for each other so that you may be healed. The prayer of a righteous person is powerful and effective. Elijah was a human being, even as we are. He prayed earnestly that it would not rain, and it did not rain on the land for three and a half years. Again he prayed, and the heavens gave rain, and the earth produced its crops. My brothers and sisters, if one of you should wander from the truth and someone should bring that person back, remember this: Whoever turns a sinner from the error of their way will save them from death and cover over a multitude of sins. (James. 5:13–20)*

Renewal & Revival

When a community of people all begin to abide in the Spirit and live out of His power, the foundation is laid for renewal and revival. Just as we have discussed, there needs to be personal regeneration (through the resurrection life of the Spirit), transformation (through the sanctifying work of the Spirit), and then ongoing abiding and empowerment through the Spirit. When this happens among many believers in a local area or church, the Body of Christ is built up and the kingdom of God begins to advance in that region. The renewing work happening within the church seeps into the larger culture and city. As the church prays, fasts, and seeks the presence and power of God, the Holy Spirit responds to the cry of His people. "After they prayed, the place where they were meeting was shaken. And they were all filled with the Holy Spirit and spoke the word of God boldly" (Acts 4:31).

When the Holy Spirit pours Himself out upon His people, spiritual awakening occurs in a city. Awakening is when God supernaturally accelerates the spread of His kingdom—when spiritual, social, and cultural renewal kick into overdrive and people respond to the gospel in increasing numbers. It's when the Holy Spirit moves through His people freely and with power as the gospel is proclaimed boldly, the sick are healed, the hungry are fed, the gifts of the Spirit flow out of God's people to build up the body, and those far from God repent and turn to Jesus. It is the kingdom of God breaking out so that the city begins to look a lot like heaven on earth.

Here at Church of the City, the cry of our heart is from Habakkuk 3:2: "Lord, I have heard of Your fame; I stand in awe of Your deeds, Lord. Repeat them in our day…" We want to see the fame and deeds of God known in our city and on the earth. We want the revivals and awakenings we have heard about—the revivals in first-century Antioch and among the Moravians in the 1700s, the Great Awakening in the 1730s, the 1850s NYC businessmen revivals, the Second Awakening in the USA, or the revival in the Hebrides in 1949—to happen again in our city. We want this to happen again in our time. We long for the day when God's presence is experienced palpably by the residents of New York City and our entire city is transformed.

To that end, we are committed as a church to praying, worshipping, fasting, discipling, evangelizing, and contending with God for spiritual awakening in our time and in our city. This is why we established a prayer room for daily hours of prayer (and one day 24/7 prayer and worship). This is why we have monthly worship nights where we cry out for revival. This is why we want to be Spirit-filled Christians who proclaim the gospel with boldness and who move out in faith as the Spirit empowers us for ministry. We long for the Presence of God in our city and spiritual awakening in our time.

Lord, may Your kingdom come and Your will be done in this city as it is in heaven. May Your fame and deeds be known in this generation. Amen.

Growing in your Identity

As we learned in this chapter, God does not invite us to follow Him and live the Christians life in our own strength, but rather out of the Spirit's power and presence. Based on your initial self-evaluation in the Introduction, here are some practical next steps for growing in your experience of the Spirit's power at work in and through your life.

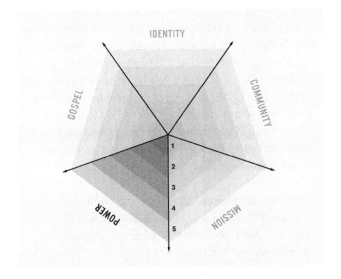

- **Know God's Plan:** If the ideas in this chapter were new to you, then the best place to start is by studying and meditating upon the Scripture passages that teach about the person and power of the Holy Spirit. Do you know and experience God as Father, Son, and Spirit? What is your level of understanding of abiding, empowerment, and experiencing God's presence? Begin memorizing verses that relate to these three main topics.

- **Experience:** If the ideas in this chapter are not new to you, but you have never experienced the filling and empowering work of the Holy Spirit before, then your next step is to invite the Spirit to fill you. Practice listening for the Spirit's voice and obeying His instructions. Ask Him to fill you with His love and power. As you do this, begin comparing days spent in step with the Spirit and days spent living out of your own strength. Practice "spiritual breathing" whenever you recognize that you have started living that day out of your own strength.

❸ **Apply:** If you have experienced the Spirit's work in your life, continue applying the lessons in this chapter to your life. Seek to abide in the Spirit's power and presence each day, learning to listen to His voice and obey Him. Discover your spiritual gifts and begin serving in the church. Grow in the practice of the spiritual disciplines. Learn to step out in bold faith asking God to move in power through you to declare the gospel and heal the sick. Lean into prayer and worship as you learn to bask in the presence of God.

❹ **Grow in Confidence:** As you grow in confidence in living out of God's power, make abiding and empowered living your new normal. Develop a "rule of life" to help you walk in the power of the Spirit throughout your day and year; include rhythms of worship, prayer, intimacy, abiding, service, and mission. Grow in confidence in your spiritual gifts, serving consistently in the ministries God has called you to. Share the gospel with joy and confidence, and move out in power knowing that God can heal the sick and free the prisoner. Let the Spirit move through you with ease, responding promptly to His rebuke, guidance, and leading.

Self Reflection:
Acts 2

This week use T.I.M.E.,
described in the Introduction,
with Acts 2.

Acts 2:1–21 (NIV)

¹ *When the day of Pentecost came, they were all together in one place.*
² *Suddenly a sound like the blowing of a violent wind came from heaven
and filled the whole house where they were sitting.* ³ *They saw what
seemed to be tongues of fire that separated and came to rest on each of
them.* ⁴ *All of them were filled with the Holy Spirit and began to speak
in other tongues as the Spirit enabled them.* ⁵ *Now there were staying in
Jerusalem God-fearing Jews from every nation under heaven.* ⁶ *When
they heard this sound, a crowd came together in bewilderment, because
each one heard their own language being spoken.* ⁷ *Utterly amazed, they
asked: "Aren't all these who are speaking Galileans?* ⁸ *Then how is it
that each of us hears them in our native language?* ⁹ *Parthians, Medes
and Elamites; residents of Mesopotamia, Judea and Cappadocia,
Pontus and Asia,* ¹⁰ *Phrygia and Pamphylia, Egypt and the parts of
Libya near Cyrene; visitors from Rome* ¹¹ *(both Jews and converts to
Judaism); Cretans and Arabs—we hear them declaring the wonders of
God in our own tongues!"* ¹² *Amazed and perplexed, they asked one
another, "What does this mean?"* ¹³ *Some, however, made fun of them
and said, "They have had too much wine."* ¹⁴ *Then Peter stood up with
the Eleven, raised his voice and addressed the crowd: "Fellow Jews
and all of you who live in Jerusalem, let me explain this to you; listen
carefully to what I say.* ¹⁵ *These people are not drunk, as you suppose.
It's only nine in the morning!* ¹⁶ *No, this is what was spoken by the
prophet Joel:* ¹⁷ *"'In the last days, God says, I will pour out my Spirit on
all people. Your sons and daughters will prophesy, your young men will
see visions, your old men will dream dreams.* ¹⁸ *Even on my servants,
both men and women, I will pour out my Spirit in those days, and they
will prophesy.* ¹⁹ *I will show wonders in the heavens above and signs on
the earth below, blood and fire and billows of smoke.* ²⁰ *The sun will be
turned to darkness and the moon to blood before the coming of the great
and glorious day of the Lord.* ²¹ *And everyone who calls on the name of
the Lord will be saved.'* [Joel 2:28–32]*

Text

Read through the above passage three times. Underline or highlight any words or phrases that jump out to you.

What phrases in this passage relate to the Spirit's Power? (*List those verses or phrases below.*)

Immerse

Choose two or three phrases or verses to study further.
You might want to look up the definition for those words,
find out where those Greek words are used elsewhere
in the Scriptures, or study the theological and historical
context for those verses. Write a summary of your findings
below and then choose one verse to memorize this week.

PHRASE A:

INSIGHT:

PHRASE B:

INSIGHT:

PHRASE C:

INSIGHT:

MEMORY VERSE:

Ministry

Now that you have read and studied the text, what is the Spirit leading you to believe or do as a result? Why did the Spirit highlight those phrases or words? What is He trying to teach you about His people? How is He calling you to live and act as a result?

Encounter

With all of this in mind, take this to God in prayer. Use the space below to write out a prayer and also to write out anything you hear God saying as a result. Then close your time by writing out a song/poem of praise to God.

MY PRAYER:

LISTENING:

MY SONG OF PRAISE:

§

Conclusion

"I have come that they may have life, and have it to the full."
—John 10:10

Jesus became a man, lived a perfect life, died a terrible death, and rose victorious from the dead so that we might have LIFE—deep, abundant, joyful, faith-filled, purposeful, rich, communal, eternal life in Him. We are not meant to live off the dregs, but to experience a rich life in Him. Jesus offers us this life by abiding in Him—believing the good news of the gospel, receiving a new and holy identity from Him, being knit together into the people of God, being sent out on God's mission to bring His kingdom, and being filled with the power of the Holy Spirit.

Growing in the way of Jesus is a life-long journey, but you can begin it today. Today, you can respond to His voice and follow Him. Today, you can lay aside your former ways of thinking and living, and instead choose to yoke yourself to Jesus as you conform your life to His teachings and practices.

This book is just the beginning.

We hope that you will return to it each year as you seek to know, experience, and grow confident in the gospel of Jesus Christ, your identity as a child of God, Christian community, God's mission, and the Spirit's power. Each year, take the self-assessments again and plan the next growth steps in your faith journey. Find a CORE group to hold you accountable and to rejoice with you when you accomplish your next step. The Christian life is not meant to be lived alone, so choose today to walk alongside others.

Our prayer for you is that you would continue to live in the way of Jesus for the renewal of our city, seeking to grow in your experience of the gospel, your understanding of your identity, your trust in Christian community, your passion for God's mission, and your reliance upon the power of the Spirit. Like the apostle Paul, we pray that:

> ... *out of His glorious riches He may strengthen you with power through His Spirit in your inner being, so that Christ may dwell in your hearts through faith. And I pray that you, being rooted and established in love, may have power, together with all the Lord's holy people, to grasp how wide and long and high and deep is the love of Christ, and to know this love that surpasses knowledge— that you may be filled to the measure of all the fullness of God.*
>
> *Now to Him Who is able to do immeasurably more than all we ask or imagine, according to His power that is at work within us, to Him be glory in the church and in Christ Jesus throughout all generations, for ever and ever! Amen.* (Eph. 3:16—21)

Sincerely,
Suzy Silk & Jon Tyson

§

Appendix A
Identity Verses

- I am faithful *(Ephesians 1:1)*
- I am God's child *(John 1:12)*
- I have been justified *(Romans 5:1)*
- I am Christ's friend *(John 15:15)*
- I belong to God *(1 Corinthians 6:20)*
- I am a member of Christ's Body *(1 Corinthians 12:27)*
- I am assured all things work together
  for good *(Romans 8:28)*
- I have been established, anointed,
  and sealed by God *(2 Corinthians 1:21–22)*
- I am confident that God will perfect the work He has
  begun in me *(Philippians 1:6)*
- I am a citizen of Heaven *(Philippians 3:20)*
- I am hidden with Christ in God *(Colossians 3:3)*
- I have not been given a spirit of fear, but of power,
  love, and self-discipline *(2 Timothy 1:7)*
- I am born of God and the evil one
  cannot touch me *(1 John 5:18)*
- I am blessed in the heavenly realms with every
  spiritual blessing *(Ephesians 1:3)*

- I am seated with Christ in
  the heavenly realms *(Ephesians 2:6)*
- I have been shown the incomparable riches of God's
  grace *(Ephesians 2:7)*
- God has expressed His kindness to me *(Ephesians 2:7)*
- I am God's workmanship *(Ephesians 2:10)*
- I have been brought near to God through Christ's
  blood *(Ephesians 2:13)*
- I have peace *(Ephesians 2:14)*
- I have access to the Father *(Ephesians 2:18)*
- I am a member of God's household *(Ephesians 2:19)*
- I am secure *(Ephesians 2:20)*
- I am a holy temple *(Ephesians 2:21; 1 Corinthians 6:19)*
- I am a dwelling for the Holy Spirit *(Ephesians 2:22)*
- I share in the promise of Christ Jesus *(Ephesians 3:6)*
- God's power works through me *(Ephesians 3:7)*
- I can approach God with freedom
  and confidence *(Ephesians 3:12)*
- I am growing *(Colossians 2:7)*
- I am His disciple *(John 13:15)*
- I am prayed for by Jesus Christ *(John 17:20–23)*
- I am united with other believers *(John 17:20–23)*
- I am not in want *(Philippians 4:19)*
- I possess the mind of Christ *(1 Corinthians 2:16)*
- I am promised eternal life *(John 6:47)*
- I am promised a full life *(John 10:10)*
- I am victorious *(1 John 5:4)*
- My heart and mind is protected
  with God's peace *(Philippians 4:7)*
- I am chosen and dearly loved *(Colossians 3:12)*
- I am blameless *(1 Corinthians 1:8)*
- I am set free *(Romans 8:2; John 8:32)*
- I am crucified with Christ *(Galatians 2:20)*
- I am overcoming *(1 John 4:4)*
- I am persevering *(Philippians 3:14)*
- I am protected *(John 10:28)*

- I am chosen before the creation of the world *(Ephesians 1:4, 11)*
- I am holy and blameless *(Ephesians 1:4)*
- I am adopted as his child *(Ephesians 1:5)*
- I am given God's glorious grace lavishly and without restriction *(Ephesians 1:5, 8)*
- I am in Him *(Ephesians 1:7; 1 Corinthians 1:30)*
- I have redemption *(Ephesians 1:8)*
- I am forgiven *(Ephesians 1:8; Colossians 1:14)*
- I have purpose *(Ephesians 1:9 & 3:11)*
- I can understand what God's will is *(Ephesians 5:17)*
- I am God's coworker *(2 Corinthians 6:1)*
- I am a minister of reconciliation *(2 Corinthians 5:17–20)*
- I am alive with Christ *(Ephesians 2:5)*
- I am raised up with Christ (*Ephesians 2:6; Colossians 2:12)*
- I am the salt and light of the earth *(Matthew 5:13–14)*
- I have been chosen and God desires me to bear fruit *(John 15:1, 5)*
- I know there is purpose for my sufferings *(Ephesians 3:13)*
- I can grasp how wide, long, high, and deep Christ's love is *(Ephesians 3:18)*
- I am completed by God *(Ephesians 3:19)*
- I can bring glory to God *(Ephesians 3:21)*
- I have been called *(Ephesians 4:1; 2 Timothy 1:9)*
- I can give thanks for everything *(Ephesians 5:20)*
- I don't have to always have my own agenda *(Ephesians 5:21)*
- I can honor God through marriage *(Ephesians 5:22–33)*
- I can parent my children with composure *(Ephesians 6:4)*
- I can be strong *(Ephesians 6:10)*
- I have God's power *(Ephesians 6:10)*
- I can stand firm in the day of evil *(Ephesians 6:13)*
- I am dead to sin *(Romans 1:12)*
- I am a personal witness of Jesus Christ *(Acts 1:8)*
- I can be humble, gentle, patient, and lovingly tolerant of others *(Ephesians 4:2)*

- I am born again *(1 Peter 1:23)*
- I am a new creation *(2 Corinthians 5:17)*
- I am delivered *(Colossians 1:13)*
- I am redeemed from the curse
  of the Law *(Galatians 3:13)*
- I am qualified to share
  in His inheritance *(Colossians 1:12)*
- I am victorious *(1 Corinthians 15:57)*
- I have hope *(Ephesians 1:12)*
- I am included *(Ephesians 1:13)*
- I am sealed with
  the promised Holy Spirit *(Ephesians 1:13)*
- I am a saint *(Ephesians 1:18)*
- I can mature spiritually *(Ephesians 4:15)*
- I can be certain of God's truths and the lifestyle
  which he has called me to *(Ephesians 4:17)*

§

Appendix B
Group Discussion Guides

Introduction

- Welcome everyone to the group. Share names, why you are here, and what you hope to get from this study.
- Read the Introduction.
- As a group, spend time taking the self-evaluation. Give people five minutes of quiet reflection and then ask them to share their evaluation with the group.
- Spend time praying for each person and the journey God is taking them on.
- Do an example version of T.I.M.E. with Ephesians 3:16–19. Walk through the four steps using this passage as an example. Give each person a chance to silently practice that step for a minute or two and then answer any questions they may have.
- *Homework: Read "Gospel" in preparation for your next group, completing the self-evaluation and T.I.M.E. included in that chapter.*

Gospel

- As a group, practice memorizing the short two-sentence version of the gospel. Any lingering questions or confusion? Which parts do you tend to forget?
- Share with one another the part of this chapter that was most meaningful for you. Which part of the good news was truly good news for you this past week?
- Share with one another your self-evaluation and action steps for this part of the pentagon. What steps will each person take this week? How can you encourage and assist each other on this journey?
- Share with one another any insights from T.I.M.E. ~ John 3.
- *Homework: Memorize the two-sentence gospel definition and read "Identity" in preparation for your next group.*

Identity

- Group Discussion: How has our culture and your upbringing formed your identity thus far? How does this compare to how God defines good, values you, and defines your identity?
- As a group, read Appendix A out loud. Which verses regarding your identity are most surprising? Encouraging? Challenging to believe? Where is God working to transform your identity?
- Share with one another your self-evaluation and action steps for this part of the pentagon. What steps will each person take this week? How can you encourage and assist each other on this journey?
- Share with one another any insights from T.I.M.E. ~ Ephesians 1.
- *Homework: Read "Community" in preparation for your next group.*

Community

- Group Discussion: What has been your experience of community in the past? What has been your experience of Christian community? Where have you struggled to find and build lasting community in the city?
- Discuss the "Building Community" section of this chapter. What are some of the joys of building a holy community? How can your group lean into the 4Ps: Priority, Practices, Proximity, and Permanence?
- Share with one another your self-evaluation and action steps for this part of the pentagon. What steps will each person take this week? How can you encourage and assist each other on this journey?
- Share with one another any insights from T.I.M.E. ~ 1 Peter 2.
- *Homework: Read "Mission" in preparation for your next group.*

Mission

- Share with one another the people, places, and positions God has sent you to in the past and is sending you to now. How can you lean into this more fully through seeking His kingdom and stewarding your resources?
- Spend time in smaller groups praying for these people/places/positions. Contend for God's promises to these people. Listen to His leading so you can go where He is already going.
- Share with one another your self-evaluation and action steps for this part of the pentagon. What steps will each person take this week? How can you encourage and assist each other on this journey?
- Share with one another any insights from T.I.M.E. ~ Luke 10.
- *Homework: Read "Power" in preparation for your next group.*

Power

- Open the group with extended prayer and worship—inviting God's Spirit to be present and move in power.
- Share with one another your spiritual gifts and how you have witnessed God's Spirit move in and through you in the past. (Take the gifts assessment if people are unfamiliar with their gifts.) Lay hands on one another and pray for greater freedom and anointing.
- Share with one another your self-evaluation and action steps for this part of the pentagon. What steps will each person take this week? How can you encourage and assist each other on this journey?
- Share with one another any insights from T.I.M.E. ~ Acts 2.
- *Homework: Read the Conclusion & complete Appendix C in preparation for your next group.*

Conclusion

- As a group, summarize the next steps you each want to take to grow in these five values. Write them out and commit to praying for one another. How can you continue to encourage and hold each other accountable?
- Using Appendix C, give each person in the group a chance to share their ten-minute testimony. Listen for patterns in their life and affirm the ways God is moving in and through them.

§

Appendix C
Writing Your Testimony

God is a God of history who "works all things for the good of those He loves" (Rom. 8:28). Before you were born, "all the days ordained for you were written in God's book" because "you are God's workmanship, created in Christ Jesus, for good works which God prepared in advance for you to do" (Ps. 139:16, Eph. 2:10). God knows your story—the highs and lows of your life, the beautiful moments, and the painful experiences—and He wants to redeem all of this for His glory and your good. Your past experiences are not wasted but can be used to bless others and worship God.

Understanding and sharing our stories is an integral part of growing in the gospel, identity, and mission. In our post-modern world, one of the easiest ways to share the good news of Jesus is through our own experience of the gospel. Understanding how God has uniquely created us is part of living out of our God-given identity. Joining God in His mission to renew all things is connected to the story God is writing in our lives—the good works He has prepared in advance for us to do.

One way to begin evaluating our past experiences is by charting our life story with a timeline (an idea first created by Viktor Frankl). Begin by filling in the life events sections. Be sure to include the events that led you to know Jesus as your Lord and Savior. Next, chart these points on the timeline, looking for patterns. Finally, write out your whole story in a ten-minute format and a three-minute format, focusing on the transformation you have experienced in Jesus.

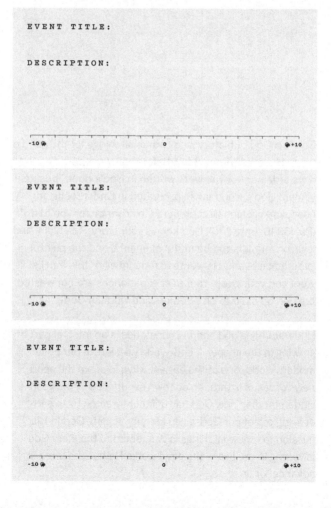

EVENT TITLE:

DESCRIPTION:

-10   0   +10

EVENT TITLE:

DESCRIPTION:

-10   0   +10

EVENT TITLE:

DESCRIPTION:

-10   0   +10

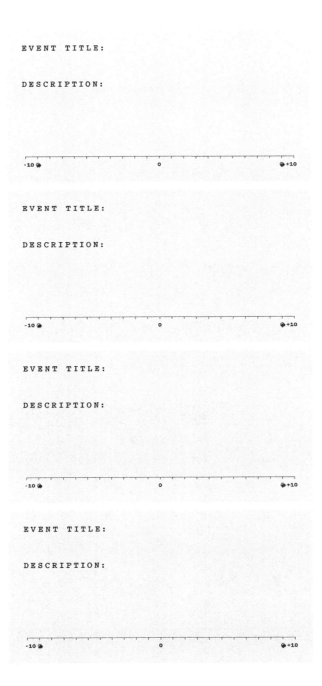

EVENT TITLE:

DESCRIPTION:

-10   0   +10

EVENT TITLE:

DESCRIPTION:

-10   0   +10

EVENT TITLE:

DESCRIPTION:

-10   0   +10

EVENT TITLE:

DESCRIPTION:

-10   0   +10

+10 ●

+9

+8

+7

+6

+5

+4

+3

+2

+1

0 ————————————————————————————————————

-1

-2

-3

-4

-5

-6

-7

-8

-9

-10 ●

§

Appendix D
Works Cited

Augustine, *The City of God*, trans. Rev. Marcus Dods (Edinburgh: T & T Clark, 1888).

"The Loneliness Experiment." Narrated by Claudia Hammond. All in the Mind. *BBC Radio 4*, October 1, 2018. https://www.bbc.co.uk/mediacentre

Bonhoeffer, Dietrich. *Life Together: The Class Exploration of Christians Community.* New York: Harper & Row Publishers, 1954.

Brown, Colin, ed.. *The New International Dictionary of New Testament Theology,* Volume 2, 107. Grand Rapids, MI: Zondervan, 1976.

Cole, Neil. Church 3.0: *Upgrades for the Future of the Church.* San Francisco, CA: Jossey-Bass, 2010.

Coleman, Robert E. *The Master Plan of Evangelism.* Grand Rapids, MI: Baker Publishing, 1963.

De Beaufort, Joseph, comp.. *The Practice of the Presence of God by Brother Lawrence.* Infinity Publishing, 2015.

Erickson, Millard. *Introducing Christian Doctrine.* Grand Rapids, MI: Baker Academic, 1992.

Erikson, Erik. *Crisis of Identity* (1968).

Fossum, Merle A. and Marilyn J. Mason. *Facing Shame: Families in Recovery.* New York: W. W. Norton & Company, 1986.

Frankl, Viktor. *The Doctor and the Soul: An Introduction to Logotherapy* (1946).

Frost, Michael and Alan Hirsch. "Foreword" in *Sentness*, by Kim Hammond and Darren Cronshaw, pages of chapter. Downers Grove, IL: Intervarsity Press, 2014.

Janzen, David. *The International Christian Community Handbook: For Idealists, Hypocrites, and Wannabe Disciples of Jesus.* Brewster, MA: Paraclete Press, 2013.

Keller, Tim. Live talk.

Kinnaman, David and Roxanne Stone. "Competing Worldviews Influence Today's Christians." Barna Group. May 9, 2017. https://www.barna.com/research/competing-worldviews-influence-todays-christians.

L'Engle, Madeline L'Engle. *A Circle of Quiet.* New York: Farrar, Straus, & Giroux, 1972.

Lewis, C. S. *The Four Loves.* New York: Harcourt Books, 1960.

Lewis, C. S. *The Screwtape Letters.* C. S. Lewis Pte. Ltd., 1942.

Mann, Alann. *Atonement for a Sinless Society.* Carlisle, UK: Paternoster Publishing, 2005.

Meyers, Joyce. "Finding Peace and Joy by Living the Simple Life." *The Christian Post.* April 6. https://www.christianpost.com/news/find-peace-and-joy-by-living-the-simple-life.html.

Moody, D. L. *The Secret of Success in the Christian Life.* Chicago, IL: Moody Press, 1881.

Murray, Andrew. *Holy in Christ.* Christian Focus Publications, 2005.

Nourwen, Henri. *Making All Things New: An Invitation to the Spiritual Life.* New York, NY: Macmillan, 1982.

Olson, Randy S. "144 Years of Marriage and Divorce in 1 Chart." Randel S. Olson. June 15, 2015. www.randalolson.com.

Piper, John. "Christian Hedonism: Forgive the label, but don't miss the truth." In *Desiring God*, 1/1/1995.

Silvoso, Ed. *Prayer Evangelism.* Grand Rapids, MI: Baker Publishing Group, 2000.

Smedes, Lewis B. "Controlling the Unpredictable: The Power of Promising." *Christianity Today.* January 21, 1983.

Swoboda, A. J. *The Subversive Sabbath: The Surprising Power of Rest in a Nonstop World.* Grand Rapids, MI: Brazos Press, 2018.

Taylor, Charles. *Sources of the Self: The Making of the Modern Identity.* Cambridge, MA: Harvard University Press, 1989.

Tennyson, Alfred. "In Memoriam A.H.H." 1849.

Tozer, A. W. *The Pursuit of God.* Christian Publications, Inc:
    1948.

Tyson, Jon. *Sacred Roots.* Grand Rapids, MI: Zondervan, 2013.

Willard, Dallas. *The Divine Conspiracy: Rediscovering Our
    Hidden Life in God.* New York: HarperOne, 2018.

Willard, Dallas. *Renovation of the Heart.* Colorado Springs,
    CO: NavPress, 2002.

Wright, N. T. *Scripture and the Authority of God.* United
    Kingdom: The Society for Promoting Christian
    Knowledge, 2005.

Yancey, Phillip. Church: *Why Bother?: My Personal
    Pilgrimage.* Grand Rapids, MI: Zondervan, 1998.

Zacharias, Ravi. Interview with Gordon Roberton. "What
    Makes the Christian Message Unique?" CBN.com.

Made in the USA
Middletown, DE
12 November 2022

14778483R00130